MODERN PUBLISHING'S

IS THAT YOUR FINAL ANSWER?

VOLUME 2

MODERN PUBLISHING
A Division of Unisystems, Inc.
New York, New York 10022
Series UPC: 39850

In *Is That Your Final Answer?*, trivia buffs
will find hundreds of questions to test
their knowledge of history, science, literature,
art, sports, movies, music, and many more topics.
Challenging and fun, the questions in
Is That Your Final Answer? will show you
just how much you know, and how much
you don't know! Whether you enjoy these
brain-teasing questions on your own or with
a group of friends, *Is That Your Final Answer?*
is a must for anyone who loves facts, figures,
history, and a good challenge. And when you are
through with *Is That Your Final Answer? Volume 2*,
you'll find more stimulating trivia questions in
Is That Your Final Answer? Volume 1. No trivia
buff should be without them.

1.

How many planets are in our solar system?
a) 7
b) 8
c) 9
d) 10

2.

Where was U.S. president William McKinley assassinated in 1901?
a) Macon, Georgia
b) Reno, Nevada
c) Buffalo, New York
d) Silver Springs, Maryland

3.

In the zodiac, Taurus is also known as
a) the Bull
b) the Ram
c) the Fish
d) the Lion

4.

On which continent can the kangaroo be found?
a) Asia
b) Europe
c) Australia
d) South America

5.

The word aphelion refers to the point in a planet's orbit when it is
a) farthest from the sun
b) nearest earth
c) farthest from earth
d) nearest the sun

6.

Which state is known as the Constitution State?
a) Connecticut
b) Pennsylvania
c) Virginia
d) Delaware

7.

What is the chief mandate of OPEC?
a) legislate fair trade practices
b) attempt to set world oil prices by controlling its production
c) regulate online activity
d) set international monetary standards

8.

Whose likeness is pictured on the $50 U.S. Savings Bond?
a) George Washington
b) Paul Revere
c) Alexander Hamilton
d) Thomas Jefferson

9.

Which of these common plants are poisonous?
a) daffodil
b) azalea
c) hyacinth
d) all of the above

10.

How many continents are there on earth?
a) 5
b) 6
c) 7
d) 8

11.

Which is totally independent from birth?
a) human
b) sea turtle
c) dog
d) bear

12.

How many cups are in a quart?
a) 2
b) 4
c) 6
d) 8

13.

Which is a symbol of Judaism?
a) Star of David
b) Agnes Dei
c) Shiva
d) Lotus

14.

What is a palette?
a) a range of colors
b) the roof of the mouth
c) a portable platform
d) all of the above

15.

Which direction do the portraits on all U.S. coins, except the Lincoln cent, face?
a) left
b) right

16.

Abraham Lincoln is portrayed on the front of which denomination of U.S. currency?
a) $5
b) $1
c) $10
d) $20

17.

Which is the farthest from New York City by airplane?
a) Geneva
b) Athens
c) Rome
d) Tel Aviv

18.

When did the first great age of exploration begin?
a) Dark Ages
b) Renaissance
c) Middle Ages
d) none of the above

19.

Which alphabet is used by the visually impaired to be able to read?
a) Cyrillic
b) Latin
c) Braille
d) Judaic

20.

Which is not a worldwide environmental crisis?
a) ozone hole
b) greenhouse effect
c) pine beetles
d) acid rain

21.

Where are the triceps muscles located in the human body?
a) upper legs
b) shoulder
c) upper arms
d) back

22.

What is considered to be a customary tip for a room-service waiter?
a) 5% of the bill
b) 10% of the bill
c) 15% of the bill
d) none of the above

23.

What is the capital city of Texas?
a) Dallas
b) Austin
c) San Antonio
d) Houston

24.

Where is the International Boxing Hall of Fame?
a) New York
b) New Jersey
c) Massachusetts
d) Pennsylvania

25.

Which famous TV doctor went on to become the star of the TV mini-series *Shogun*?
a) Vince Edwards
b) Richard Chamberlain
c) James Brolin
d) Robert Young

26.

How are asteroids and comets like planets?
a) they revolve around the sun
b) they have satellites
c) they revolve around the earth
d) they travel at the speed of light

27.

Which is not a baby horse?
a) pony
b) colt
c) foal
d) filly

28.

If you use the 24-hour system to tell time, what is 1400 equal to?
a) 1 p.m.
b) 2 p.m.
c) 3 p.m.
d) 4 p.m.

29.

Which is not a branch of mathematics?

a) arithmetic

b) semantics

c) geometry

d) algebra

30.

Where were the first public libraries built?

a) Rome

b) Greece

c) Egypt

d) none of the above

31.

Which is not a continent?

a) Poland

b) Europe

c) Asia

d) Africa

32.

Where is Washington State?

a) north of Oregon

b) south of Oregon

c) east of Montana

d) none of the above

33.

How many bones are in the human body?
a) 106
b) 206
c) 306
d) none of the above

34.

Where is the deltoid muscle?
a) shoulder
b) leg
c) stomach
d) neck

35.

During which activity do you expend the most calories?
a) driving
b) standing
c) typing
d) sitting

36.

Which is closest to New York by airplane?
a) St. Croix
b) Caracas
c) Bermuda
d) San Jose

37.
What is the name of the currency used in Angola?
a) dollar
b) peso
c) kwanza
d) dinar

38.
What was the name of the mission that launched the first human into orbital flight?
a) Vostok
b) Gemini
c) Virgo
d) Soyuz

39.
What is the capital city of California?
a) San Francisco
b) Los Angeles
c) Sacramento
d) Fresno

40.
Which TV entertainer was known for the saying, "How sweet it is"?
a) Mike Douglas
b) Jackie Gleason
c) Caesar Romero
d) Drew Carey

41.

Who is portrayed on the front of a twenty dollar bill?
a) Andrew Jackson
b) John Adams
c) Zachary Taylor
d) James Buchanan

42.

In 1968, Senator Robert F. Kennedy was shot and killed in Los Angeles. Who was convicted of the crime?
a) James Earl Ray
b) Sirhan Sirhan
c) John W. Hinckley, Jr.
d) Mark Chapman

43.

How many phases are there to the moon?
a) 3
b) 4
c) 5
d) 6

44.

Which continent is the smallest of those listed?
a) Antarctica
b) Australia
c) South America
d) Africa

45.

On which continent is Libya?
a) South America
b) Africa
c) Europe
d) Asia

46.

Which activity, done at a vigorous pace, expends the least calories?
a) bicycling
b) rowing
c) running
d) basketball

47.

Who won the 1906 Nobel Peace Prize?
a) Theodore Roosevelt
b) the International Red Cross
c) Woodrow Wilson
d) none of the above

48.

Which illness is not caused by a virus?
a) mumps
b) malaria
c) measles
d) the common cold

49.

During whose presidency did the Bay of Pigs incident occur?
a) Dwight D. Eisenhower
b) Lyndon B. Johnson
c) John F. Kennedy
d) Richard Nixon

50.

A tadpole is a baby
a) fish
b) frog
c) caterpillar
d) bird

51.

In which branch of mathematics does subtraction fall?
a) geometry
b) algebra
c) arithmetic
d) none of the above

52.

What defines *values?*
a) the lightness or darkness of a color
b) the monetary worth of something
c) a principle or ideal
d) all of the above

53.

Which healthcare specialist treats children?
a) neurologist
b) radiologist
c) dermatologist
d) pediatrician

54.

What is the most well-known case of extinction?
a) of the dinosaur
b) of the condor
c) of the dodo bird
d) of the carrier pigeon

55.

Who won the 1986 Academy Award for Best Actor for his role in *The Color of Money?*
a) Tom Cruise
b) Paul Newman
c) Michael Douglas
d) Dustin Hoffman

56.

Who were Moe, Larry, and Curly?
a) the Marx Brothers
b) the Three Stooges
c) a vaudeville act
d) Watergate informants

57.

Which is false?
a) there is no gravity on the moon
b) asteroids and comets orbit the sun
c) there are four phases to the moon
d) all of the above

58.

Which of these longest rivers in the world is the shortest?
a) Congo
b) Mekong
c) Mississippi
d) Niger

59.

Which was believed to be the largest of the meat-eating dinosaurs?
a) Tyrannosaurus
b) Deinonychus
c) Triceratops
d) Iguanodon

60.

Who devised the theory of gravity?
a) Albert Einstein
b) Isaac Newton
c) Edmund Halley
d) Galileo Galilei

61.

Which state is west of Nevada?

a) Utah

b) Arizona

c) California

d) Wyoming

62.

Which of these diseases is not caused by a virus?

a) chicken pox

b) typhus

c) polio

d) the common cold

63.

During whose presidency did the Iran hostage crisis occur?

a) Jimmy Carter

b) Ronald Reagan

c) Gerald Ford

d) Richard Nixon

64.

Which is true?

a) the currency used in Vatican City is the lira

b) New Orleans is a city in Kentucky

c) fleas and ticks are internal parasites that prey on animals

d) none of the above

65.

Which word originally referred to the area of land that an ox could plow in a day?
a) yard
b) league
c) acre
d) mile

66.

What is the word used in the United Kingdom for the American term "hood" (of a car)?
a) bonnet
b) hat
c) cap
d) muff

67.

What is another name for the card game Solitaire?
a) bridge
b) poker
c) patience
d) rummy

68.

Which is a popular song by country singer Patsy Cline?
a) Where the Boys Are
b) Somewhere
c) Stand by Your Man
d) Crazy

69.

A solar eclipse is when
a) the moon passes in front of the sun and is between it and the earth
b) when the earth comes between the sun and the moon
c) when the moon is behind the sun
d) none of the above

70.

Where are the Andes Mountains?
a) Europe
b) Alaska
c) South America
d) Australia

71.

Which was the biggest dinosaur?
a) Tyrannosaurus
b) Herrerasaurus
c) Apatosaurus
d) Seismosaurus

72.

Where were shoes invented in 2000 BC?
a) Near East
b) Europe
c) Egypt
d) Americas

73.

Which president pardoned Vietnam War draft resisters?
a) Ronald Reagan
b) Gerald Ford
c) Richard Nixon
d) Jimmy Carter

74.

Who won the 1987 Academy Award for Best Actress for her role in a movie featuring the classic opera for *La Bohéme*?
a) Meryl Streep
b) Jody Foster
c) Cher
d) Sally Field

75.

According to Catholicism, who is the Patron Saint of Ecologists?
a) St. Patrick
b) St. Francis of Assisi
c) St. Jude
d) St. Barbara

76.

Which of these diseases is caused by a virus?
a) botulism
b) hepatitis
c) malaria
d) lyme disease

77.

What is the the term used in the United Kingdom
the American word "suspenders"?

a) braces
b) belt
c) jumper
d) none of the above

78.

Who played the title role in the 1990s remake of *The
Nutty Professor*?

a) Steve Martin
b) Eddie Murphy
c) Tom Cruise
d) Kevin Costner

79.

Which is false about planets?

a) they give off light
b) they reflect light from the sun
c) planets orbit the sun
d) all of the above

80.

Which is the Greek word meaning earthquake that is also
the name for measuring the intensity of an earthquake?

a) cosmos
b) seismos
c) chrono
d) osteo

81.

Who invented blue jeans?
a) Levi Straus
b) Liz Claiborne
c) Gloria Vanderbilt
d) Calvin Klein

82.

In British peerage, which is the highest rank of heredity below a prince?
a) marquis
b) duke
c) baron
d) viscount

83.

Which are not cold-blooded animals?
a) reptiles
b) fish
c) amphibians
d) birds

84.

What is the capital of Spain?
a) Madrid
b) Barcelona
c) Cordoba
d) Toledo

85.

Where in the human body is the mandible?
a) jaw
b) ankle
c) hip
d) elbow

86.

What do olive oil, Vaseline, and burned toast have in common?
a) all can be used as home remedies
b) all can be used to cook
c) all can be used to clean
d) none of the above

87.

Which is a commonly used first aid technique for a choke victim?
a) Heimlich maneuver
b) mouth-to-mouth resuscitation
c) appendectomy
d) none of the above

88.

Which historical U.S. document begins "When in the course of human events...."?
a) the Constitution
b) the Declaration of Independence
c) the Gettysburg Address
d) the Bill of Rights

89.

Who originally recorded the hit song La Bamba?
a) Ritchie Valens
b) Buddy Holly
c) Billie Holiday
d) Gloria Estefan

90.

What is the final stage of a star called?
a) black hole
b) supernova
c) white dwarf
d) nebula

91.

Which of all the gemstones is the hardest?
a) ruby
b) emerald
c) diamond
d) garnet

92.

What is a group of bees called?
a) a cloud
b) a horde
c) a swarm
d) a grist

93.

What kind of tree is an evergreen?
a) broadleaf
b) tropical
c) coniferous
d) none of the above

94.

If you use the 24-hour system to tell time, what time is 2100 equal to?
a) 7 p.m.
b) 8 p.m.
c) 9 p.m.
d) 10 p.m.

95.

Which civilization made the first ice cream circa 2000 BC?
a) Chinese
b) Turkish
c) Irish
d) English

96.

Which president was the youngest to be elected?
a) Ronald Reagan
b) John F. Kennedy
c) Gerald Ford
d) Jimmy Carter

97.

Who was the first American to win the World Chess title?
a) Al Unser
b) Bobby Darin
c) Bobby Fischer
d) Billie Jean King

98.

Which president of the U.S. signed a bill that made the Veteran's Administration a Cabinet department?
a) George Bush
b) Ronald Reagan
c) William Clinton
d) Richard Nixon

99.

To date, where was the highest temperature ever recorded in the U.S.?
a) Death Valley, California
b) Mojave, California
c) Los Alamos, New Mexico
d) Austin, Texas

100.

In 1872, which ship sailing from New York to Genoa, Italy, was found abandoned with loss of life unknown?
a) Princess Alice
b) Titanic
c) Stonewall
d) Mary Celeste

101.

Which player won the Women's Wimbledon
Championship six consecutive times from 1982 to 1987?
a) Martina Navratilova
b) Virginia Wade
c) Steffi Graf
d) Ann Jones

102.

From which house of rulers of England did Queen
Victoria come?
a) Hanover
b) Tudor
c) Stuart
d) York

103.

Who said, "I never met a man I didn't like"?
a) Will Rogers
b) Charlie Chaplin
c) Charles de Gaulle
d) none of the above

104.

Which is the highest peak in the world?
a) Everest
b) McKinley
c) Kilimanjaro
d) Aconcagua

105.

According to the order of British peerage, which is the lowest grade of peerage?
a) duchess
b) countess
c) viscountess
d) baroness

106.

According to the National Weather Service, which form of flooding accounts for most flood deaths in the U.S.?
a) flash flood
b) coastal flood
c) river flood
d) ice jam

107.

Which is considered to be a standard tip for a coat check attendant?
a) $1 per coat
b) $2 per coat
c) less than $1 per coat
d) none of the above

108.

Which country's national flag is red and white and features a red maple leaf?
a) Switzerland
b) Canada
c) Japan
d) none of the above

109.

Which Broadway play is based on a great novel by Victor Hugo?

a) *Miss Saigon*
b) *Les Miserables*
c) *Cats*
d) *Phantom of the Opera*

110.

What is the instrument used to see objects in space called?

a) gyroscope
b) telescope
c) binoculars
d) periscope

111.

Which is the least nutritious fruit?

a) cucumber
b) apple
c) banana
d) fig

112.

Where were potato chips invented in 1853?

a) San Francisco
b) Chicago
c) Saratoga Springs
d) Duluth

113.

Whose likeness is pictured on the $1000 U.S. Savings Bond?
a) Ben Franklin
b) Theodore Roosevelt
c) Aaron Burr
d) John Quincy Adams

114.

What do Death Valley, Gobi, and Kalahari have in common?
a) all are deserts
b) all are in the Middle East
c) all are earthquake sites
d) all are tourist attractions

115.

Who won the 1999 Stanley Cup?
a) Dallas Stars
b) Boston Bruins
c) Buffalo Sabres
d) Atlanta Thrashers

116.

Who was the 16th president of the U. S.?
a) Abraham Lincoln
b) James Buchanan
c) Lyndon B. Johnson
d) Ulysses S. Grant

117.

In case of death or impeachment who succeeds the president?
a) the speaker of the house
b) the attorney general
c) the vice president
d) the secretary of state

118.

Which of these gems is red in color?
a) topaz
b) sapphire
c) ruby
d) emerald

119.

Which is not a period in prehistory?
a) Iron Age
b) Bronze Age
c) Stone Age
d) Middle Ages

120.

Who was not a wife of Henry VIII?
a) Catherine of Aragon
b) Jane Seymour
c) Anne Boleyn
d) Elizabeth I

121.

What is considered to be a customary tip for a taxi driver?
a) 5% of the bill
b) 10% of the bill
c) 15% of the bill
d) 20% of the bill

122.

Which national flag is blue and white and features a six-pointed star?
a) Israel
b) North Korea
c) United Kingdom
d) Ghana

123.

What is the capital city of Vermont?
a) Rutland
b) Montpelier
c) Burlington
d) none of the above

124.

How many pieces does each player in a chess game get?
a) 12
b) 14
c) 16
d) 18

125.
How much time is in an *olympiad*?
a) 4 years
b) 3 years
c) 5 years
d) 2 years

126.
Who starred in the motion picture *Evita* and sang the title role?
a) Betty Buckley
b) Madonna
c) Barbara Streisand
d) none of the above

127.
How much of the earth's surface is covered with water?
a) 1/8
b) 1/4
c) 1/2
d) 3/4

128.
Which gem is the birthstone of November?
a) ruby
b) opal
c) topaz
d) garnet

129.

What do hourglasses, pendulums, and chronometers have in common?
a) all measure weight
b) all are ways to measure land
c) all measure time
d) none of the above

130.

Which is the capital city of Louisiana?
a) New Orleans
b) Shreveport
c) Baton Rouge
d) Alexandria

131.

Which female singer revealed that "All I Wanna Do" is have fun?
a) Sheryl Crow
b) Madonna
c) Cyndi Lauper
d) Jewel

132.

How many disks does each player in a game of checkers get?
a) 10
b) 12
c) 14
d) 16

133.

In U.S. military time, what time is it if it is 2300 hours?
a) 10 p.m.
b) 11 p.m.
c) 12 p.m.
d) 12 p.m.

134.

How many cards are in a standard Pinochle deck?
a) 44
b) 46
c) 48
d) 50

135.

Where in the human body is the Eustachian tube?
a) nose
b) throat
c) ear
d) eyes

136.

In the zodiac, Gemini is also known as
a) the Crab
b) the Water Bearer
c) the Twins
d) the Scales

137.

Where does the most rain occur in the U.S. and the world?

a) Mount Everest, Nepal
b) Mount Waialeale, Hawaii
c) Death Valley, California
d) Amazon Jungle

138.

Who declined to accept the 1964 Nobel Prize in Literature?

a) Jean-Paul Sartre
b) John Steinbeck
c) Heinrich Böll
d) Pablo Neruda

139.

What is the name of the award given to the best show in Broadway theater?

a) Tony Award
b) Emmy Award
c) Golden Globe
d) Academy Award

140.

Who said "Give me liberty or give me death"?

a) Patrick Henry
b) Benedict Arnold
c) Alexander Hamilton
d) George Washington

141.

Which state was not one of the 13 original states?
a) Pennsylvania
b) Massachusetts
c) New York
d) Kentucky

142.

Of all the 11 states that seceded from the Union, which was the last to be readmitted after the Civil War?
a) Tennessee
b) Alabama
c) Georgia
d) Texas

143.

In the movie *The Godfather*, who played the elder Vito Corleone?
a) Robert de Niro
b) Marlon Brando
c) Paul Newman
d) Burgess Meredith

144.

Which is the smallest of the four oceans?
a) Atlantic
b) Pacific
c) Indian
d) Arctic

145.

Which is the oldest continuously used calendar in history?
a) Babylonian
b) Mayan
c) Egyptian
d) Chinese

146.

In which country was the first hamburger cooked?
a) France
b) Spain
c) United States
d) Germany

147.

In which style of art are objects shown as geometric shapes?
a) Impressionism
b) Fauvism
c) Cubism
d) Realism

148.

Where was the first dictionary compiled?
a) Greece
b) Egypt
c) China
d) Europe

149.

Who invented the magnifying lens in 1250?
a) Ben Franklin
b) Roger Bacon
c) Jules Verne
d) none of the above

150.

By what name was Catherine II—Empress of Russia—known?
a) the Fair
b) the Great
c) the Beguiled
d) the Brave

151.

For which month is a sapphire the gemstone?
a) October
b) September
c) December
d) January

152.

Which is the most nutritious fruit?
a) apple
b) pear
c) avocado
d) lime

153.

Who built the first "skyscraper" in 1882?
a) William Le Baron Jenny
b) Frank Lloyd Wright
c) Leonardo da Vinci
d) Robert Mills

154.

In which TV western was Artemis Gordon a government agent?
a) *Gunsmoke*
b) *High Chaparral*
c) *Wild, Wild West*
d) *Big Valley*

155.

After calling for his pipe and his bowl, what did Old King Cole want?
a) his wisdom tree
b) his fiddler's three
c) a trip to the sea
d) none of the above

156.

Which early civilization of people lived as city dwellers in the jungles of Central America?
a) Aztec
b) Mayan
c) Incan
d) none of the above

157.

Which explorer conquered the Incan civilization?
a) Pizarro
b) Cortes
c) Magellan
d) da Gama

158.

In this popular children's song, if you "*row, row, row your boat,*" life is supposed to be this
a) an adventure
b) a nightmare
c) a dream
d) a long journey

159.

What are an igloo, log cabin, skyscraper, and teepee examples of?
a) art
b) architecture
c) literature
d) music

160.

What are ordinal numbers?
a) when you skip count
b) when you count consecutively
c) when you put numbers in place order
d) when you count backwards

161.

Which evil pirate had his hand bitten off by a crocodile?
a) Bluebeard
b) Captain Hook
c) Jean Lafitte
d) Davy Jones

162.

Which is not a living thing?
a) animal
b) mineral
c) plant
d) none of the above

163.

Who was the first U.S. Secretary of the Treasury?
a) Alexander Hamilton
b) Ben Franklin
c) Francis Scott Key
d) Thomas Jefferson

164.

What word describes the political system of Europe during the Middle Ages?
a) futile
b) feudal
c) fertile
d) none of the above

165.

If something is moving at supersonic speed, it is moving faster than
a) a bullet
b) the speed of light
c) the speed of sound
d) none of the above

166.

Which children's TV show featured a talking moose and a silent rabbit?
a) *Romper Room*
b) *Captain Kangaroo*
c) *Sesame Street*
d) *The Soupy Sales Show*

167.

According to the nursery rhyme, what will happen *when the wind blows?*
a) the cradle will rock
b) the clock will tock
c) the door will lock
d) the sitter will knock

168.

Who was Yuri I. Gagarin?
a) a physicist
b) a Soviet official
c) the first human launched into orbital flight
d) a novelist

169.

Where are all 10 of the highest mountains in the U. S. located?
a) Alaska
b) Colorado
c) Utah
d) California

170.

Which president ordered the Lewis and Clark Expeditions of 1804?
a) Thomas Jefferson
b) James Madison
c) Ulysses S. Grant
d) James Monroe

171.

In mythology, what race of giants inhabited earth before man?
a) Cyclops
b) Gorgons
c) Titans
d) none of the above

172.

Which early civilization of people were known as cruel conquerors, forcing the people they ruled to become human sacrifices to their gods?
a) Incan
b) Mayan
c) Aztec
d) Aleutian

173.

Which popular song did Mozart—one of the greatest composers of all time—like to play?
a) Row, Row, Row Your Boat
b) Twinkle, Twinkle Little Star
c) I've Been Working on the Railroad
d) none of the above

174.

What do these have in common: fish, lion, eagle, and ladybug?
a) all are animals
b) all are mammals
c) all are cold blooded
d) all make their own food

175.

Which nationality was Jonathan Swift, author of the classic story *Gulliver's Travels?*
a) English
b) Irish
c) German
d) Belgian

176.

Which period of history came first?
a) Bronze Age
b) Stone Age
c) Iron Age
d) Middle Ages

177.

Which is not a movie starring Warren Beatty?

a) *Reds*

b) *Shampoo*

c) *Bonnie and Clyde*

d) *Tightrope*

178.

Where was the king when four and twenty blackbirds were baked in a pie?

a) on his throne

b) sleeping

c) in the counting house

d) dining

179.

Where did the early civilization known as the Incas live?

a) high in the Andes Mountains

b) high in the Rocky Mountains

c) high in the Alps

d) high in the Appalachian Mountains

180.

In which ship did the Pilgrims arrive in 1620?

a) Nina

b) Pinta

c) Mayflower

d) Santa Maria

181.

Who was the king of Ancient Greece?
a) Socrates
b) Alexander
c) Attila
d) Caesar

182.

Who portrayed the U.S. president in the movie
Absolute Power?
a) Clint Eastwood
b) Gene Hackman
c) Robert Redford
d) Martin Sheen

183.

Which word refers to the point at which a planet's
orbit is nearest the earth?
a) perigee
b) apogee
c) aphelion
d) perihelion

184.

Who was warned by his/her mother to stay out of Mr.
McGregor's garden?
a) Peter Rabbit
b) Mopsy
c) Flopsy
d) all of the above

185.

When Christopher Columbus set sail from Europe, where did he think he was going?
a) Australia
b) America
c) Asia
d) Antarctica

186.

Whose likeness is pictured on the $5000 U.S. Savings Bond?
a) Alexander Hamilton
b) John Adams
c) Woodrow Wilson
d) Paul Revere

187.

Which style of music was born in America?
a) classical
b) jazz
c) folk
d) all of the above

188.

In which early period of time did art begin?
a) Bronze Age
b) Stone Age
c) Iron Age
d) Ice Age

189.

In which movie did Ann Bancroft play Annie Sullivan, Helen Keller's teacher?
a) *Miracle on 34th Street*
b) *The Miracle Worker*
c) *The Miracle of the Bells*
d) *The Miracle Woman*

190.

Which story is not a fable by Aesop?
a) The Hare and the Tortoise
b) The Fox and the Grapes
c) The Wind and the Sun
d) The Ugly Duckling

191.

Which country did Queen Isabella and King Ferdinand rule?
a) France
b) Spain
c) England
d) Portugal

192.

Which group arrived in America first?
a) Puritans
b) Amish
c) Pilgrims
d) Shakers

193.

Who were the sea-going warriors that raided Europe during the Middle Ages?
a) Crusaders
b) Vikings
c) Normans
d) Spartans

194.

The 1965 movie *Doctor Zhivago* is based on a novel by
a) Boris Pasternak
b) Ernest Hemingway
c) William Faulkner
d) Raymond Carver

195.

When Paul Revere arranged the signal "One if by land, two if by sea," what did it refer to?
a) lamps in a window
b) horses in a field
c) birds in a cage
d) crop circles in a field

196.

Who wrote the novel that the movie *War of the Worlds* is based on?
a) Orson Welles
b) H. G. Wells
c) Jules Verne
d) Sir Arthur Conan Doyle

197.

In which decade did the Great Depression occur?
a) 1920s
b) 1930s
c) 1940s
d) none of the above

198.

What type of pasta is used in baked ziti?
a) ziti
b) rigatoni
c) spinach noodles
d) egg noodles

199.

What were dinosaurs?
a) amphibians
b) mammals
c) reptiles
d) crustaceans

200.

The FBI is the law enforcement branch of
a) The Dept. of Justice
b) The Dept. of Commerce
c) The Dept. of Transportation
d) The Internal Revenue Service

201.

In 1679, which city was the first to hire firefighters?
a) Boston
b) Philadelphia
c) New York
d) Williamsburg

202.

Which is not a vertebrate?
a) fish
b) bat
c) octopus
d) human

203.

Which duo provided background vocals for Tony Orlando?
a) Donny and Marie
b) Sony and Cher
c) Dawn
d) Ike and Tina Turner

204.

Which of Santa's reindeer had a red nose?
a) Rudolph
b) Blitzen
c) Donder
d) Cupid

205.

The fictional character Peter Pan, who lived in Neverland, was leader of
a) the Beastie Boys
b) the Lost Boys
c) the Green Mountain Boys
d) none of the above

206.

How long is China's Great Wall?
a) almost 1000 miles
b) almost 4000 miles
c) almost 2000 miles
d) none of the above

207.

Which monument contains a sign with a poem that begins, "Give me your tired, your poor..."?
a) Lincoln Memorial
b) Washington Monument
c) Statue of Liberty
d) Jefferson Memorial

208.

In the song Do-Re-Mi, what is La
a) a long, long way to run
b) a drop of golden sun
c) a deer, a female deer
d) a note to follow so

209.

James Hoban is famous because he was the
a) architect of the White House
b) architect of the Chrysler Building
c) architect of the Flatiron Building
d) architect of the Sears Tower

210.

Who was the architect of the Guggenheim Museum in New York City?
a) Frank Lloyd Wright
b) Paul Rudolph
c) Louis Skidmore
d) William Strickland

211.

What was Ansel Easton Adams famous for?
a) photographing landscapes of the American Southwest
b) photographing Depression-era children
c) establishing a museum of photography
d) being a WPA photographer

212.

Which is the highest peak in the U. S.?
a) McKinley
b) Washington
c) Lincoln
d) Shasta

213.

What water formation is the largest body of fresh water in the world?
a) the Great Lakes
b) Niagara Falls
c) Lake Victoria
d) Lake Mead

214.

On June 15, 1752, who proved that lightning was electricity?
a) Ben Franklin
b) Paul Revere
c) Abe Lincoln
d) Marconi

215.

Who, by opening a box, unleashed multiple plagues on man?
a) Pandora
b) Prometheus
c) Aristotle
d) Kronus

216.

In which year did the ship *Titanic* hit an iceberg and sink in the North Atlantc?
a) 1912
b) 1918
c) 1928
d) 1942

217.

Does a cyclone rotate clockwise or counterclockwise in the southern hemisphere?
a) clockwise
b) counter clockwise

218.

Who was the Russian monk assassinated in 1916?
a) Kirov
b) Pushkin
c) Rasputin
d) Danton

219.

In Internet lingo, what is a window?
a) an application
b) a screen saver
c) a new document
d) a portion of the screen that contain its own document

220.

From which house of rulers of England did Henry VIII come?
a) Tudor
b) York
c) Stuart
d) Hanover

221.

What is the official beginning of the third millennium?
a) December 31, 2000
b) December 31, 1999
c) January 1, 2001
d) January 31, 2001

222.

What invention in the year 1250 was the precursor to all optical instruments?
a) binoculars
b) magnifying glass
c) contact lens
d) bifocal

223.

As of December 31, 1999, the Panama Canal is controlled by
a) Panama
b) Cuba
c) United States
d) Canada

224.

According to the saying, what does *absence* make the heart do?
a) grow fonder
b) beat harder
c) stop
d) get lonely

225.

Where is the highest mountain in the world?
a) Nepal/Tibet
b) United States
c) Switzerland
d) France

226.

Which Hollywood star appeared in the most movies?
a) John Wayne
b) Ronald Reagan
c) Errol Flynn
d) Troy Donahue

227.

Who said, "Adversity makes a man, prosperity makes monsters"?
a) Charles Dickens
b) Victor Hugo
c) Franklin D. Roosevelt
d) Jean-Paul Sartre

228.

Who was one of the greatest physicists of all time?
a) Andre Ampere
b) Max Born
c) Albert Einstein
d) David Brewster

229.
Where is Mount Kilimanjaro?
a) Africa
b) Alaska
c) France
d) Asia

230.
Which is not one of the Great Lakes?
a) Superior
b) Michigan
c) Huron
d) Mead

231.
Who was the top-scoring champion in basketball for seven years in a row, from 1960 to 1966?
a) Wilt Chamberlain
b) Bob Pettit
c) Neil Johnston
d) Elvin Hayes

232.
How many books are in the New Testament?
a) 25
b) 27
c) 31
c) 20

233.

In the Bible, who was Abraham's son?
a) Isaac
b) Esau
c) Jacob
d) Adam

234.

Who was the 1983 Women's Wimbledon Champion?
a) Steffi Graf
b) Martina Navratilova
c) Tracy Austin
d) Billie Jean King

235.

What does the Greek prefix *cosmo-* mean?
a) universe
b) magazine
c) city
d) none of the above

236.

Who is Maya Angelou?
a) a modern American writer
b) a model
c) a TV host
d) a painter

237.

Where did 80,000 prospectors go in 1849 to look for gold?
a) California
b) Colorado
c) Texas
d) New Mexico

238.

Which river is the longest in the world?
a) Amazon
b) Mississipi
c) Nile
d) Congo

239.

In Internet lingo, what does IMO stand for?
a) in my opinion
b) an electrical unit
c) an international monetary organization
d) a chat group

240.

John Steinbeck's novel about the effect the Great Depression had on a family was titled
a) *The Grapes of Wrath*
b) *Of Mice and Men*
c) *Travels with Charley*
d) *East of Eden*

241.

Which holiday in the U.S. is usually celebrated on the third Sunday of June?
a) Flag Day
b) Memorial Day
c) Father's Day
d) Citizenship Day

242.

Who appoints the justices for the U.S. Supreme Court?
a) the president of the U.S.
b) the attorney general
c) the speaker of the house
d) the vice president

243.

Who is the author of *Prometheus Bound?*
a) Sophocles
b) Plato
c) Euripides
d) Aeschylus

244.

Which animals can reproduce asexually, that is, when only one parent creates the offspring?
a) flatworm
b) coral
c) sponges
d) all of the above

245.

Where was the yo-yo invented in approximately 1100 BC?
a) China
b) Europe
c) the Americas
d) the South Pacific

246.

In 1953, with whom did Sir Edmund Hillary ascend to the top of Mount Everest, becoming the first people in history to do so?
a) Tenzing Norgay
b) Henry Hunt
c) Reinhold Messner
d) none of the above

247.

Muhammed, the prophet, founded which religion that holds the Koran as its sacred text?
a) Buddhism
b) Judaism
c) Islam
d) Taoism

248.

Who led the Chicago Bulls to six championships and retired in 1999?
a) Patrick Ewing
b) Kobe Bryant
c) Michael Jordan
d) Shaquille O'Neal

249.

In what year were the Winter Olympic Games started?
a) 1924
b) 1925
c) 1936
d) 1937

250.

What is *half a loaf* better than?
a) a coupon
b) none
c) a bird in the hand
d) a roll

251.

What is the greenhouse effect?
a) the melting of the Polar ice caps
b) when you keep houseplants
c) a special effect technique
d) none of the above

252.

Which parent corporation owns these consumer brands:
Almond Joy, Kit Kat candy bar, and Ronzoni pasta?
a) Hershey Food Corp.
b) Sara Lee
c) The Gap
d) Proctor and Gamble

253.

Where was magnetism first discovered circa 60 AD?
a) China
b) Ukraine
c) Egypt
d) Greece

254.

Who won the XXVII and XXVIII Super Bowl games?
a) Dallas Cowboys
b) Greenbay Packers
c) San Francisco 49ers
d) Miami Dolphins

255.

Where is the Empire State Building located?
a) San Francisco
b) Chicago
c) New York City
d) Phoenix

256.

According to the proverb, which city "wasn't built in a day"?
a) Paris
b) New York
c) Rome
d) Madrid

257.

During which epoch of the Cenozoic Era did humans evolve?

a) Miocene
b) Pleistocene
c) Oligocene
d) none

258.

Sophocles, the Greek playwright, wrote

a) *Antigone*
b) *Julius Ceasar*
c) *Romeo and Juliet*
d) *The Tempest*

259.

Which event took place first?

a) the Boston Tea Party
b) the invention of the telephone
c) the discovery of electricity
d) the Civil War

260.

What service ended on October 24, 1861, with the completion of the first transcontinental telegraph line?

a) Federal Express
b) Pony Express
c) United Postal Service
d) none of the above

261.

Who caused King Arthur's downfall?
a) Modred, his kinsman
b) a dragon
c) the Crusades
d) the bubonic plague

262.

What is the Roman name for the Greek goddess Athena?
a) Minerva
b) Diana
c) Hera
d) Ciro

263.

During which decade was the Charleston a social dance?
a) 1910s
b) 1920s
c) 1930s
d) 1950s

264.

In which U.S. time zone is the state of North Carolina?
a) Eastern Time
b) Central Time
c) Pacific Time
d) Mountain Time

265.

What are aleph, het, and nun?
a) letters from the Hebrew alphabet
b) the names of Roman gods
c) figures from Greek mythology
d) letters from the Latin alphabet

266.

What did Robert Fulton invent in 1807?
a) rail car
b) steamboat
c) combustion engine
d) printing press

267.

Grandma Moses was
a) a farmer's wife who began painting in her 70s
b) a physicist
c) an engineer
d) a nurse

268.

Who first believed that the sun was the center of the universe?
a) Halley
b) Copernicus
c) Apollo
d) Plato

269.

El Greco, one of the best-known artists from Spain, is well known for his paintings in which theme?
a) still life
b) self portrait
c) religious ecstasy
d) mural

270.

Which became the 49th state of the U.S.?
a) Tennessee
b) Alabama
c) Alaska
d) Texas

271.

Where did Carlo Collodi, the author of *Pinocchio*, come from?
a) Germany
b) France
c) Spain
d) Italy

272.

What is the world's most important yacht race?
a) Whitbread Race
b) BOC Race
c) America's Cup
d) America Alone Race

273.

Which three are notable African-Americans of the 20th Century?
a) Colin L. Powell
b) Maya Angelou
c) Marian Anderson
d) George Washington Carver

274.

What is the Federal statute of limitations—the time limitation during which charges can be brought against someone for a crime or offense that is not a capital offense?
a) 2 years
b) 5 years
c) 4 years
d) 3 years

275.

Which president carved into Mount Rushmore is wearing a monocle?
a) Abraham Lincoln
b) Thomas Jefferson
c) Theodore Roosevelt
d) George Washington

276.

What is the English Channel?
a) a TV broadcasting station in Great Britain
b) a narrow portion of the Atlantic Ocean
c) a narrow portion of the Pacific Ocean
d) a group of parapsychologists

277.

How many are in a baker's dozen?
a) 12
b) 13
c) 14
d) 15

278.

Who was a great movie comedian?
a) Arthur Fiedler
b) W.C. Fields
c) Rachel Field
d) none of the above

279.

Who founded the Mormon religion?
a) Joseph Smith
b) Brigham Young
c) John Calvin
d) Martin Luther

280.

Who was Louis Armstrong?
a) a world-renowned trumpet player
b) a world-class tennis champion
c) a classical musician
d) a jazz pianist

281.

By what name was William I of the House of
Normandy known?
a) the Conqueror
b) the Confessor
c) the Martyr
d) the Glorious

282.

Who invented frozen food?
a) Sara Lee
b) Birdseye
c) Campbell
d) Heinz

283.

Of the four National Parks listed, which receives the
fewest visitors each year?
a) Grand Canyon
b) Lake Mead
c) Statue of Liberty
d) Blue Ridge Parkway

284.

Of the four, which is not a daughter of Zeus?
a) Aphrodite
b) Hera
c) Artemis
d) Athena

285.

What was Muhammad Ali's birth name?

a) Sonny Liston
b) Leon Spinks
c) Cassius Clay
d) none of the above

286.

Which are the only mammals that can fly?

a) owls
b) birds
c) bats
d) crows

287.

Which magical land did author L. Frank Baum create?

a) Shangri-la
b) Oz
c) Valhalla
d) Nirvana

288.

Which is the largest carnivore in North America?

a) wolf
b) moose
c) bear
d) mountain lion

289.

Where is the world's largest railway tunnel?
a) Japan
b) United Kingdom-France
c) Italy
d) United States

290.

In what year was Beatrix Potter's *The Tales of Peter Rabbit* first published?
a) 1900
b) 1905
c) 1910
d) 1915

291.

What is the passage of water that separates Alaska from Asia and is where a land bridge enabled peoples to migrate to the Americas during the Ice Age?
a) Trans-Isthmian Canal
b) Straight of Gibralter
c) Bering Straight
d) Gulf Stream

292.

Which is not a warm-blooded animal?
a) eagle
b) rabbit
c) snake
d) dog

293.

Which was the first state to legalize boxing?
a) New Jersey
b) California
c) Illinois
d) New York

294.

Which basketball center was the only one in the history of the game to score 100 points in a game?
a) Kareem Abdul Jabbar
b) Michael Jordan
c) Larry Bird
d) Wilt Chamberlain

295.

Who was the creator and host of the original *Candid Camera* TV show?
a) Allen Funt
b) Sid Caesar
c) Bill Cosby
d) Steve Allen

296.

Who is one of the most popular fictional characters, created by Edgar Rice Burroughs?
a) Superman
b) Batman
c) Tarzan
d) Mr. Spock

297.

What are Monarch, Tiger Swallowtail, and Cabbage White?
a) birds
b) butterflies
c) fresh water fish
d) salt water fish

298.

Which one of the seven wonders of the ancient world can still be visited?
a) the Hanging Gardens of Babylonia
b) the Olympian Zeus
c) the Pyramids of Egypt
d) the Colossus of Rhodes

299.

Which country forms the northern border of the U.S.?
a) Newfoundland
b) Mexico
c) Nova Scotia
d) Canada

300.

In the U.S. Constitution, which amendment gave women the right to vote?
a) 13th
b) 15th
c) 19th
d) none of the above

301.

Who invaded China in the 13th Century, building the most expansive empire as he did so?
a) Genghis Khan
b) Attila the Hun
c) Napoleon
d) Hannibal

302.

What was the Black Death also known as?
a) bubonic plague
b) chicken pox
c) measles
d) polio

303.

Who was the president of the Confederacy of the southern states that seceded from the U. S. just before the Civil War began?
a) Robert E. Lee
b) Jefferson Davis
c) "Stonewall" Jackson
d) J. E. B. Stuart

304.

What is the protection and wise use of natural resources known as?
a) environmentalism
b) conservation
c) federalism
d) naturalism

305.

Where is the Great Divide in the U.S.?
a) Appalachian Mountains
b) Rocky Mountains
c) Adirondack Mountains
d) Blue Ridge Mountains

306.

How many inches are in a square foot?
a) 60
b) 125
c) 85
d) 144

307.

To whom did Constantinople fall in 1453?
a) the Ottoman Turks
b) the Cathars
c) the Crusaders
d) none of the above

308.

Where is the home of the Grand Ole Opry?
a) Nashville, Tennessee
b) Macon, Georgia
c) New Orleans, Lousiana
d) Gainesville, Florida

309.

Who were Crazy Horse and Sitting Bull?
a) Watergate informants
b) great leaders of Native American peoples in the U.S.
c) comedians
d) Native American actors

310.

What was the most famous song recorded by Bing Crosby?
a) Swinging On a Star
b) White Christmas
c) Alexander's Ragtime Band
d) I'll Be Home for Christmas

311.

Whose expedition reached the New World in 1492?
a) Christopher Columbus
b) Amerigo Vespucci
c) Vasco da Gama
d) Hernan Cortes

312.

Which event precipitated the French Revolution?
a) the revocation of the Edict of Nantes
b) the Glorious Revolution
c) the storming of the Bastille
d) the Seven Years' War

313.

What do Martin Scorsese, Orson Welles, and Stanley Kubrick have in common?
a) all graduated from Harvard
b) all are famous financiers
c) all are renowned movie directors
d) all have degrees in economics

314.

Which two buildings in the U.S. are the same number of stories tall, although they are not the same height?
a) the Sears Tower in Chicago, Illinois
b) the Empire State Building in New York
c) the Chrysler Building in New York
d) the World Trade Center buildings in New York

315.

Which dam in the U.S. is on the Nevada-Arizona border?
a) San Luis Dam
b) Fort Peck Dam
c) Hoover Dam
d) Grand Coulee Dam

316.

What was D-Day?
a) the allied invasion of German-occupied France
b) the end of World War I
c) the end of World War II
d) the German invasion of France

317.

Grand Canyon State is the nickname of which state?
a) Arizona
b) Utah
c) Montana
d) Idaho

318.

In which movie did Victor Mature play the title role?
a) *The Ten Commandments*
b) *Samson and Delilah*
c) *American Gigolo*
d) *Some Like It Hot*

319.

In U.S. politics, who was the speaker of the house from 1995 to 1999?
a) Janet Reno
b) Madeleine Albright
c) Newt Gingrich
d) John Podesta

320.

James Earl Ray was the convicted assassin of
a) Robert Kennedy
b) John F. Kennedy
c) John Lennon
d) Reverend Dr. Martin Luther King, Jr.

321.

At what longitude is the International Date Line set?
a) 180 degrees
b) 185 degrees
c) 188 degrees
d) 190 degrees

322.

How old is Methuselah, the oldest living tree in the U.S., believed to be?
a) 1000 years
b) 2500 years
c) 4700 years
d) 250 years

323.

What is Edward Jenner known as?
a) a triathlon-winning athlete
b) discoverer of the vaccine for small pox
c) a TV newscaster
d) a Broadway actor

324.

Where was Napoleon defeated in 1815?
a) Paris
b) Nice
c) Normandy
d) Waterloo

325.

What is the nickname of Texas?
a) the Lone Star State
b) the Mountain State
c) the Keystone State
d) the Buckeye State

326.

Whose assassination sparked World War I?
a) Austrian Archduke Franz Ferdinand
b) German Kaiser Wilhelm III
c) France's Napoleon III
d) Prussia's Otto von Bismarck

327.

Who was Secretary of State during the Kennedy administration?
a) Dean Rusk
b) Richard Nixon
c) Henry Kissinger
d) Edmund S. Muskie

328.

From which house of rulers of England does Elizabeth II come?
a) Stuart
b) Hanover
c) York
d) Windsor

329.

Who invented the floppy disk in 1970?
a) IBM
b) Sony
c) RCA
d) Microsoft

330.

Who won the 1993 Nobel Prize in Literature?
a) Toni Morrison
b) John Updike
c) Stephen King
d) Joyce Carol Oates

331.

Which state is also known as the Golden State?
a) Missouri
b) Alaska
c) California
d) Texas

332.

Whose likeness is pictured on the $100 U.S. Savings Bond?
a) Alexander Hamilton
b) Thomas Jefferson
c) George Washington
d) Abraham Lincoln

333.

Which U.S. coin was the first to have the motto "In God We Trust" engraved on it?
a) Lincoln penny
b) two cent coin of 1864
c) Indian head nickel
d) Eisenhower dime

334.

What are APO, MVP, and ZIP samples of?
a) acronyms
b) synonyms
c) antonyms
d) none of the above

335.

What does *magna cum laude* mean?
a) with great distinction
b) with great achievement
c) with great merit
d) with great praise or honor

336.

Who did the first commemorative coin produced in the U.S. honor?
a) Christopher Columbus
b) Pizarro
c) Ponce de Leon
d) Abraham Lincoln

337.

In which direction does the portrait of Lincoln face on the one-cent coin?
a) right
b) left

338.

What do Ernest Hemingway, Eugene O'Neill, and George Bernard Shaw have in common?
a) all received a Nobel Prize in Literature
b) all are British
c) all are poets
d) all studied at Oxford

339.

Which honor is given to the author of the most distinguished book in American literature for children?
a) Nobel Prize
b) Caldecott Medal
c) Pulitzer Prize
d) Newbery Medal

340.

Which U.S. denomination of currency has Ben Franklin on the front?
a) $100
b) $50
c) $20
d) $1000

341.

What is the highest military award for bravery given in the U.S.?
a) the Bronze Star
b) the Purple Heart
c) the Silver Star
d) the Medal of Honor

342.

Who was the first American in space?
a) Alan B. Shepard, Jr.
b) John H. Glenn, Jr.
c) M. Scott Carpenter
d) Edwin "Buzz" Aldrin, Jr.

343.

The fifty dollar bill has Ulysses S. Grant on the front and which national landmark on the back?
a) the U.S. Capitol Building
b) the Lincoln Memorial
c) Independence Hall
d) the White House

344.

Who was the first American to orbit Earth?
a) John H. Glenn, Jr.
b) Edwin "Buzz" Aldrin, Jr.
c) M. Scott Carpenter
d) Alan B. Shepard, Jr.

345.

What do the cheetah, whooping crane, and Asian elephant have in common?
a) all inhabit southeast Asia
b) all are endangered species
c) all are from the order Marsupialia
d) all are herbivores

346.

What is the average lifespan of a grizzly bear?
a) 25 years
b) 10 years
c) 5 years
d) 60 years

347.

Which animal is the fastest runner?
a) lion
b) antelope
c) cheetah
d) mule deer

348.

Which honor is given to the illustrator of the most distinguished American picture book for children?
a) Christopher Award
b) Kate Greenaway Medal
c) Caldecott Medal
d) Bologna Prize

349.

Which classic movie won the 1943 Academy Award for Best Picture?
a) *Casablanca*
b) *Rebecca*
c) *Gentleman's Agreement*
d) *The Lost Weekend*

350.

What do the black mamba, puff adder, and boomslang have in common?
a) all are venomous snakes
b) all are rap stars
c) all are names of popular dances
d) all are gang leaders

351.

Which major U.S. public zoological park has the most acres?
a) Bronx Zoo
b) San Diego Wild Animal Park
c) San Francisco Zoo
d) Detroit Zoological Park

352.

Of the top 50 dog breeds listed by the American Kennel Club, which ranked #1 in popularity for 1997 and 1998?
a) Labrador Retriever
b) German Shepherd
c) Akita
d) Beagle

353.

What is the name of the oldest living tree in the U.S.?
a) Old Glory
b) Ironside
c) Methuselah
d) Intrepid

354.

Which 1998 movie grossed the most dollars?
a) *Saving Private Ryan*
b) *Titanic*
c) *Enemy of the State*
d) *Lethal Weapon 4*

355.

To date, which is the longest running show on New York's Broadway?
a) *Fiddler on the Roof*
b) *Carousel*
c) *Cats*
d) *Chorus Line*

356.

In which year did John H. Glenn, Jr. orbit the earth three times?
a) 1959
b) 1960
c) 1961
d) 1962

357.

As of 1998, which of the world's airports had the most passenger arrivals and departures?
a) Heathrow
b) JFK
c) Charles De Gaulle
d) Tokyo International

358.

Which city is the home of the National Aviation Hall of Fame?
a) New Paltz, New York
b) Denver, Colorado
c) Dayton, Ohio
d) Naples, Florida

359.

What are *Alpha, Bravo, and Charlie* examples of?
a) International Radio Alphabet
b) Watergate informants
c) names of roses
d) names of stars

360.

What is the layer of atmosphere closest to the earth known as?
a) troposphere
b) stratosphere
c) ionosphere
d) thermosphere

361.

In which year did the Wright Brothers make their historic flight near Kitty Hawk, North Carolina?
a) 1903
b) 1900
c) 1910
d) 1905

362.

Who was the first flight attendant?
a) Ellen Church
b) Ellen Kirk
c) Elaine Clark
d) Eleanor Hearn

363.

When was the sound barrier broken by Chuck Yeager?
a) 1947
b) 1900
c) 1924
d) 1950

364.

Which picture won the 1944 Academy Award for Best Picture?
a) *Going My Way*
b) *The Best Years of Our Lives*
c) *Hamlet*
d) *Mrs. Miniver*

365.

What does the phrase *summa cum laude* mean?
a) with the highest praise or honor
b) with the highest merit
c) with the highest achievement
d) with the highest distinction

366.

What are AWOL, DNA, and FYI samples of?
a) synonyms
b) acronyms
c) antonyms
d) homophones

367.

Baby fox are called
a) kits
b) cubs
c) pups
d) all of the above

368.

What was the most popular boy's name for five decades, from 1950 to 1998?
a) James
b) Michael
c) Dennis
d) John

369.

What is the commonly used French phrase that means one has a zest for life?

a) carpe diem
b) c'est la vie
c) joie de vivre
d) que sera sera

370.

What is a violent rotating column of air with winds of over 200 mph that reaches from the ground to a cumulonimbus cloud above?

a) severe thunderstorm
b) tornado
c) hurricane
d) tropical storm

371.

What do these names have in common: Isak Dinesen, George Eliot, and George Sand?

a) they are all pen names used by women authors
b) they are all British
c) they are all poets
d) they are all politicians

372.

What was the real name of popular author Mark Twain?

a) Samuel Clemens
b) Stewart Clemens
c) Clement Samuels
d) Clementine Hunt

373.

Which three are commonly misspelled words in the English language?
a) commitment
b) embarrass
c) millennium
d) forever

374.

What is a hurricane called west of the International Date Line?
a) typhoon
b) tornado
c) tropical storm
d) cyclone

375.

How many inches of rain falls annually on the rainiest place on earth: Mount Waialeale, Hawaii?
a) 200 inches
b) 460 inches
c) 130 inches
d) 85 inches

376.

Which steamer was torpedoed in 1915 and sunk by a German submarine?
a) *The General Slocum*
b) *Titanic*
c) *Lusitania*
d) *Stonewall*

377.

Where did the worst accident in the history of nuclear power occur?
a) Los Alamos
b) Three Mile Island
c) Chernobyl
d) Nagaski

378.

Who assassinated President Lincoln in 1865?
a) John Wilkes Booth
b) James Earl Ray
c) Sirhan Sirhan
d) none of the above

379.

Which parent corporation owns these consumer brands: Coach leather goods, Playtex Apparel, and Hanes Hosiery?
a) Proctor and Gamble
b) Sara Lee
c) Gillette
d) The Gap

380.

What is the chief mandate of NATO?
a) to regulate international arms practices
b) to legislate fair trade practices
c) to settle disputes peacefully and come to member nations' defense if necessary
d) to establish an international code of ethics

381.

Where will the 2000 World's Fair be held?
a) United States
b) Germany
c) France
d) Spain

382.

Which president of the U.S. was assassinated by Charles J. Gaiteau in 1881?
a) James A. Garfield
b) Rutherford B. Hayes
c) Chester A. Arthur
d) Grover Cleveland

383.

How much time is in a fortnight?
a) one week
b) two weeks
c) three weeks
d) four weeks

384.

Which word refers to the point in a planet's orbit when it is nearest to the sun?
a) perihelion
b) apogee
c) perigee
d) aphelion

385.

When a remnant of material, ice, or rock falls from space to the ground on earth, it is called a
a) meteorite
b) meteor
c) comet
d) meteroid

386.

In the Zodiac, Aries is also known as
a) the Scales
b) the Twins
c) the Ram
d) the Fish

387.

What was the name of the German zeppelin that burned in 1937?
a) *Hindenburg*
b) *Graf Zeppelin*
c) *Led Zeppelin*
d) *Graf Zeppelin II*

388.

How much time is in a millennium?
a) 100,000 years
b) 100 years
c) 1000 years
d) 1 million years

389.

What is the name of the day when the sun is farthest from the equator?
a) solstice
b) equinox
c) daylight savings
d) eclipse

390.

In the Zodiac, Cancer is also called
a) the Crab
b) the Lion
c) the Rabbit
d) the Fish

391.

Which of these islands is the largest?
a) Greenland
b) Great Britain
c) Sumatra
d) Borneo

392.

Who discovered the Pacific Ocean?
a) Magellan
b) Balboa
c) Columbus
d) Da Gama

393.

Who was Britain's longest reigning monarch?

a) Elizabeth I
b) Victoria
c) Edward VIII
d) none of the above

394.

Where in the body is the patella located?

a) ankle
b) wrist
c) knee
d) elbow

395.

Who starred in the Oscar-winning movie *All About Eve*?

a) Bette Davis
b) Joan Crawford
c) Myrna Loy
d) Merle Oberon

396.

Which is not considered to be a social science?

a) geography
b) anthropology
c) economics
d) nutrition

397.

In the Zodiac, Leo is also known as
a) the Scales
b) the Lion
c) the Twins
d) the Archer

398.

Where were cosmetics invented in the year 3750 BC?
a) China
b) Egypt
c) Mesopotamia
d) Greece

399.

Where did the first passenger railway open in 1831?
a) England
b) United States
c) France
d) Italy

400.

What do notchback, fastback, and hatchback refer to?
a) types of whales
b) shapes of cars
c) names of motorcycles
d) football players

401.

During which king's reign in France was ballet recognized as a form of art?
a) Louis XIV
b) Philip V
c) Charles X
d) Henry III

402.

Which famous painter designed sets for the Alfred Hitchcock classic film, *Spellbound?*
a) Pablo Picasso
b) Salvador Dali
c) Joseph Cornell
d) Mark Rothko

403.

What is the mission of the U.S. Head Start Program?
a) to ensure every child gets an education
b) to provide healthcare to low-income families
c) to provide services to children of low-income families
d) to establish daycare programs

404.

Which sign of the Zodiac is the Archer known as?
a) Sagittarius
b) Libra
c) Gemini
d) Aquarius

405.

Which is the longest bone in the human body?
a) femur
b) pelvis
c) humerous
d) scapula

406.

What is the field of archaeology considered to be?
a) an earth science
b) a social science
c) a life science
d) a physical science

407.

Who made the first man-powered flight, which crossed the English Channel?
a) Charles Lindbergh
b) Bryan Allen
c) Amelia Earhart
d) Chuck Yeager

408.

Which movie was the first motion picture with sound?
a) *The Birth of a Nation*
b) *The Jazz Singer*
c) *Wings*
d) *The Broadway Melody*

409.

Which was not a TV western?

a) *The Big Valley*
b) *High Chapparal*
c) *Gunsmoke*
d) *Green Acres*

410.

Who said, "Hitch your wagon to a star"?

a) Ralph Waldo Emerson
b) Henry David Thoreau
c) Oscar Wilde
d) William Blake

411.

Which sign of the Zodiac is the goat known as?

a) Aries
b) Leo
c) Capricorn
d) Scorpio

412.

Of these four deserts, which is the smallest?

a) Sahara
b) Gobi
c) Kalahari
d) Mojave

413.

Where in the body is the fibula located?
a) upper arm
b) lower leg
c) upper leg
d) foot

414.

Who played Eliot Ness in the feature film *The Untouchables?*
a) Gene Hackman
b) Kevin Costner
c) Robert De Niro
d) Robert Redford

415.

Which U.S. space probe took pictures of Neptune in 1989?
a) Voyager 2
b) Mariner 10
c) Surveyor 1
d) Venera 9

416.

How much did the first computer ENIAC, built at the University of Pennsylvania, weigh?
a) 20 tons
b) 25 tons
c) 30 tons
d) 50 tons

417.

How many signs of the Zodiac are there?
a) 10
b) 12
c) 13
d) 14

418.

Who made it possible for cars to be more affordable and available for people?
a) Eli Ransom Olds
b) Henry Ford
c) Karl Benz
d) Henry Royce

419.

Which is true about the Gossamer Albatross? It was
a) the first man-powered flight
b) a pedal-driven propeller plane
c) a historic flight across the English Channel
d) all of the above

420.

When did the supersonic airliner Concorde make its first flight?
a) 1950s
b) 1960s
c) 1970s
d) 1980s

421.

For which movie did Charles Laughton win an Academy Award for Best Actor?
a) *The Big Clock*
b) *The Canterville Ghost*
c) *Tales of Manhattan*
d) *The Man From Down Under*

422.

The patterns made by the stars are called
a) constellations
b) galaxies
c) universes
d) black holes

423.

What do Andromeda, Aquarius, and Canis Minor have in common?
a) all are constellations
b) all are names of ships
c) all are characters from mythology
d) all are models of cars

424.

Which type of cloud is usually seen in fair weather?
a) Cirrus
b) Stratus
c) Cumulus
d) all of the above

425.

Where is Cape Horn?
a) southern tip of India
b) southern tip of Africa
c) southern tip of South America
d) southern tip of Australia

426.

Of the 206 bones in the human body, where is the smallest?
a) wrist
b) ear
c) ankle
d) lips

427.

Which of these is not a film starring John Wayne?
a) *True Grit*
b) *Platoon*
c) *The Green Berets*
d) *The Searchers*

428.

What does the name of the constellation Cygnus mean?
a) swan
b) dog
c) lantern
d) flame

429.

Which branch of engineering deals with the construction of buildings, roads, and tunnels?
a) mechanical
b) electrical
c) civil
d) mining

430.

Where was the bicycle invented?
a) China
b) Egypt
c) England
d) Scotland

431.

Which monarch was the first to set up a public postal system in England?
a) Charles I
b) Henry VIII
c) Elizabeth II
d) Henry II

432.

What is Matthew Brady known as?
a) father of the Brady Bunch
b) American Civil War photographer
c) U.S. Cabinet member
d) youngest person to enter a university

433.

Who directed *The Treasure of Sierra Madre*, starring
Humphrey Bogart?
a) Elia Kazan
b) John Huston
c) John Ford
d) William Wyler

434.

When was Halley's Comet first observed?
a) 240 BC
b) 1700s
c) 1800s
d) 1900s

435.

What does the name of the constellation Draco mean?
a) dog
b) dark
c) deep
d) dragon

436.

Who starred with Mickey Rourke in the film *Barfly*?
a) Faye Dunaway
b) Sally Field
c) Shirley MacLaine
d) Linda Lavin

437.

Which painting introduced the art style of cubism?

a) *Weeping Woman*
b) *Blu di Cielo*
c) *Young Redhead in an Evening Dress*
d) *Starry Night*

438.

Which sculpture was done by Auguste Rodin?

a) *Pieta*
b) *The Thinker*
c) *David*
d) *Zeus of Olympia*

439.

Who is famous for writing limericks—five-line, rhyming nonsense poems?

a) Norman Lear
b) Edward Lear
c) Lewis Carroll
d) Oscar Wilde

440.

Which sport do *bantam, fly,* and *feather* apply to?

a) fishing
b) boxing
c) horseback riding
d) archery

441.

Although he has high hopes, *everyone knows an ant can't....*
a) climb a tree
b) cross the ocean
c) move a rubber tree plant
d) move a mountain

442.

Which is the deepest ocean trench in the world?
a) Puerto Rico Trench
b) Mariana Trench
c) Java Trench
d) none of the above

443.

How often does Halley's comet make its orbit?
a) every 50 years
b) every 100 years
c) every 76 years
d) none of the above

444.

What does the name of the constellation Orion mean?
a) Little Dog
b) the Hunter
c) Ship's Stern
d) Little Horse

445.

Where can one see the phenomenon known as the
Aurora Borealis?
a) northern hemisphere
b) southen hemisphere
c) the equator
d) Alaska

446.

Who named the constellations?
a) the Egyptians
b) the Ancient Greeks
c) the Chinese
d) the Sumerians

447.

Where is the Mojave Desert?
a) Africa
b) Asia
c) Mexico
d) United States

448.

Where is the Cape of Good Hope?
a) South America
b) India
c) Africa
d) Greenland

449.

What shape is our galaxy, the Milky Way?
a) elliptic
b) spiral
c) circular
d) triangular

450.

Who invented the thermometer?
a) Galileo
b) Franklin
c) Fermi
d) Marconi

451.

Which artist was one of the pioneers of assemblage?
a) Henri Matisse
b) Pablo Picasso
c) Georgia O'Keeffe
d) Joseph Cornell

452.

Which planet is farthest from the sun?
a) Neptune
b) Pluto
c) Uranus
d) Saturn

453.

What do Hastings, Midway, and Normandy refer to?
a) names of ships
b) major world battles
c) earthquake sites
d) military academies

454.

Of these vertebrates, which have the most developed brains?
a) amphibians
b) reptiles
c) birds
d) fish

455.

What is the spectacular natural light show that occurs in the southern skies called?
a) aurora borealis
b) aurora australis
c) star shower
d) eclipse

456.

What is the explosion that supposedly gave birth to the universe referred to as?
a) Big Bang
b) Big Boom
c) Big Noise
d) Big Bopper

457.

Which planet is closest to the sun?
a) Jupiter
b) Saturn
c) Mercury
d) Mars

458.

What can aurora refer to?
a) a colorful display of light seen near the polar region
b) a Walt Disney princess
c) the Latin word for sun
d) all of the above

459.

Which event in history occurred first?
a) the first session of the U.N. General Assembly takes place
b) the Wright Brothers make their first flight
c) there is a revolution in Russia
d) Marx and Engels publish the *Communist Manifesto*

460.

Who is best known for writing adventure stories?
a) Edgar Allan Poe
b) Rudyard Kipling
c) T.S. Eliot
d) James Joyce

461.

Who was the first woman in space?
a) Sally Ride
b) Valentina Tereskova
c) Mary Cleave
d) Christa McAuliffe

462.

What is the field of chemistry considered to be?
a) an earth science
b) a mathematical science
c) a physical science
d) a social science

463.

Moving away from the sun, which planet is past the earth?
a) Mars
b) Saturn
c) Jupiter
d) Pluto

464.

Which is the sixth planet from the sun?
a) Saturn
b) Venus
c) Mercury
d) Neptune

465.

Where is the largest space telescope known as the Hubble Space Telescope currently located?
a) in orbit around the earth
b) on Mars
c) in Washington, D.C.
d) at the Ritter Planetarium and Brooks Observatory

466.

How many moons or natural satellites does Mars have?
a) 1
b) 2
c) 3
d) 4

467.

Who discovered four of the 16 of Jupiter's moons in 1610?
a) Galileo
b) Columbus
c) Copernicus
d) Halley

468.

Which two planets have no natural satellites or moons?
a) Mercury and Venus
b) Mars and Pluto
c) Earth and Saturn
d) Jupiter and Neptune

469.

What does *biannual* mean?
a) twice a year
b) every two years
c) every two months
d) every other year

470.

Which is the symbol of Islam?
a) the Cross
b) Star and Crescent
c) Buddha
d) Menorah

471.

What is the name of the largest of Neptune's eight moons or natural satellites?
a) Caliban
b) Io
c) Triton
d) Charon

472.

The planets Uranus, Neptune, and Pluto were discovered only after
a) the telescope was invented
b) World War II
c) 1900
d) the first man walked on the moon

473.

Which is the fifth largest planet?
a) Uranus
b) Earth
c) Neptune
d) Jupiter

474.

How many layers does the earth's atmosphere have?
a) 3
b) 4
c) 5
d) 6

475.

Which is not a symbol of Taoism?
a) yin-yang
b) om
c) water
d) none of the above

476.

Which is the outermost layer of the earth's atmosphere?
a) ionosphere
b) biosphere
c) ecosphere
d) ozone

477.

According to the Chinese calendar, what is the year 2000 known as?
a) Year of the Snake
b) Year of the Dragon
c) Year of the Horse
d) Year of the Rat

478.

Which one is a symbol of Buddhism?
a) lotus
b) om
c) torii
d) yin-yang

479.

Empire State is the nickname of which state?
a) New York
b) New Jersey
c) Rhode Island
d) Massachusetts

480.

What are *Romeo, Tango,* and *Victor* samples of?
a) Shakespearean characters
b) Watergate informants
c) gang leaders
d) International Radio Alphabet

481.

What is the equivalent of 500 in Roman numerals?
a) C
b) D
c) X
d) M

482.

Which is not one of the life sciences?
a) anthropology
b) ecology
c) biology
d) medicine

483.

Where were the first operas performed?
a) Germany
b) Italy
c) France
d) Austria

484.

When was the first joint Russian-American mission in space?
a) 1970
b) 1975
c) 1980
d) 1985

485.

Which planet is the largest in our solar system?
a) Saturn
b) Venus
c) Jupiter
d) Earth

486.

Of these animals, which is the slowest runner?
a) jackal
b) wildebeest
c) coyote
d) lion

487.

In 1998, what was banned by 19 European countries?
a) human cloning
b) transplants
c) aerosol spray cans
d) recycling

488.

Which is not a physicist?
a) Albert Einstein
b) Pierre Curie
c) Christian Johann Doppler
d) Rachel Carson

489.

When was the first jet aircraft built?
a) 1920s
b) 1930s
c) 1940s
d) 1950s

490.

In Internet lingo what does CUL mean?
a) an inexperienced Internet user
b) an unsolicited e-mail
c) see you later
d) an on-screen indicator

491.

Who was a developmental psychologist?
a) Sigmund Freud
b) Carl Jung
c) Jean Piaget
d) B.F. Skinner

492.

Which of these paintings by Vincent Van Gogh sold for the highest price at auction?
a) *Irises*
b) *Sunflowers*
c) *Portrait of Dr. Gachet*
d) none of the above

493.

When was the first Indianapolis 500 race held?

a) 1911
b) 1920
c) 1930
d) 1940

494.

Which country shares the Iberian Peninsula with Spain?

a) France
b) Germany
c) Portugal
d) Italy

495.

In which movie was the theme song White Christmas first performed?

a) *Gentlemen Prefer Blondes*
b) *Holiday Inn*
c) *Top Hat*
d) *The Bells of St. Mary's*

496.

Which was the first undeclared war fought by the U.S.?

a) Civil War
b) Korean War
c) World War I
d) Vietnam War

497.

Which corporation did the FCC grant the right to first broadcast in color?
a) CBS
b) NBC
c) RCA
d) WOR

498.

Where was irrigation invented?
a) China
b) Egypt
c) Greece
d) Syria

499.

What is the popular name of the constellation Hydrus?
a) Little Dog
b) Little Snake
c) Little Lion
d) Little Bear

500.

Where was the first U.S. transcontinental railroad completed?
a) Denver, Colorado
b) Promontory Point, Utah
c) Sacramento, California
d) Salt Lake City, Utah

501.

Who was the first to introduce mass production on a moving assembly line in the U.S.?
a) Henry Ford
b) Ransom Eli Olds
c) Thomas Coleman du Pont
d) John D. Rockefeller

502.

What branch of medicine do social, experimental, and clinical relate to?
a) anatomy
b) psychology
c) rheumatology
d) oncology

503.

Which treaty, signed after World War I, established the League of Nations?
a) Treaty of Tordesillas
b) Treaty of Paris
c) Treaty of Versailles
d) Yalta Conference

504.

Which is not a poet?
a) Emily Dickinson
b) Robert Browning
c) William Blake
d) Edward Albee

505.

Which sea surrounds the eastern coastline of Italy?
a) North Sea
b) Red Sea
c) Adriatic Sea
d) Black Sea

506.

If you are playing poker, what are the odds of getting two pairs?
a) I to I
b) 20 to I
c) 46 to I
d) none of the above

507.

Which was the first film made with a stereo soundtrack?
a) *Fantasia*
b) *Gone With the Wind*
c) *The Birth of a Nation*
d) *Ben Hur*

508.

In what year was *The Star-Spangled Banner* adopted as the national anthem of the U.S.?
a) 1925
b) 1931
c) 1937
d) 1942

509.

Who was inaugurated as president after Franklin D. Roosevelt died from a cerebral hemorrhage?
a) Harry Truman
b) Dwight D. Eisenhower
c) John F. Kennedy
d) Richard Nixon

510.

Who popularized the phrase "rock 'n' roll" in 1954?
a) Cousin Brucie
b) Alan Freed
c) Wolfman Jack
d) Elvis Presley

511.

Which part of the human brain helps us balance?
a) frontal lobe
b) cerebellum
c) brain stem
d) parietal lobe

512.

What is another name for the North Star?
a) Polaris
b) Mira
c) Alpha Centauri
d) Sirius

513.

Which of these animals is the fastest runner?
a) warthog
b) squirrel
c) chicken
d) coyote

514.

What is the phobia *bibliophobia* a fear of?
a) books
b) banks
c) bats
d) blood

515.

Which is a male singing voice?
a) mezzo-soprano
b) contralto
c) soprano
d) baritone

516.

Who won the Indianapolis 500 race in 1999?
a) Al Unser, Jr.
b) Buddy Lazier
c) Kenny Black
d) Rick Mears

517.

Which is the largest country on the continent of South America?

a) Argentina
b) Brazil
c) Bolivia
d) Venezuela

518.

In which year did Broadway see a revival of burlesque with the show *Sugar Babies*?

a) 1980
b) 1981
c) 1982
d) 1983

519.

Which country-western singer was a star of the Grand Ole Opry when he was 14 years old?

a) Conrad Twitty
b) Hank Williams
c) Johnny Cash
d) George Jones

520.

Where was the windmill invented in 640?

a) India
b) Persia
c) Greece
d) China

521.

Which American artist is best known for paintings of women and children?
a) Edward Hopper
b) Mary Cassatt
c) Winslow Homer
d) Georgia O'Keeffe

522.

Who founded the Church of England?
a) King Henry VIII
b) Elizabeth I
c) Elizabeth II
d) none of the above

523.

Which of the Four Horsemen of the Apocalypse rides a white horse?
a) War
b) Famine
c) Death
d) Pestilence

524.

Who said, "Man is his own worst enemy"?
a) Confucius
b) Cicero
c) Benjamin Franklin
d) Sigmund Freud

525.

What is the official language of the country of Brunei?
a) Portuguese
b) Malay
c) French
d) Chinese

526.

Which is true?
a) a geyser is a tranquil body of water
b) thousands of species of bacteria live in a handful of soil
c) rain forests are found in the U.S.
d) none of the above

527.

Where in the human body are more than half of its bones located?
a) skull
b) hands and feet
c) legs
d) torso

528.

Who won the 1998 Grammy Award for Best Album?
a) Alanis Morissette
b) Whitney Houston
c) Lauryn Hill
d) Celine Dion

529.

During the era of Prohibition, what were clandestine places to have a drink called?
a) pubs
b) speakeasies
c) watering holes
d) basements

530.

What are igneous, metamorphic, and permeable?
a) types of clouds
b) kinds of flowers
c) types of rocks
d) none of the above

531.

Which of these musical wind instruments is in the flute family?
a) piccolo
b) bassoon
c) bass clarinet
d) saxophone

532.

Who said, "A vow is a snare for sin"?
a) Ben Franklin
b) Samuel Johnson
c) Ralph Waldo Emerson
d) Mark Twain

533.

What is the official language of the kingdom of Morocco?
a) Arabic
b) Hebrew
c) Spanish
d) Berber

534.

Which pioneer of medicine identified the virus responsible for AIDS?
a) Christiaan Barnard
b) Robert Charles Gallo
c) Albert Bruce Sabin
d) Jonas Salk

535.

For which animal does the male of the species carry the young, until they are independent?
a) kangaroo
b) koala
c) sea horse
d) whale

536.

Who is the chairman of the U.S. Federal Reserve System?
a) John Galbraith
b) Gerard Debreu
c) Alan Greenspan
d) Henry George

537.

What is the study of space and the universe called?

a) astrology
b) astronomy
c) anatomy
d) cosmology

538.

What was zoologist John James Audubon best known for?

a) ornithology
b) sociology
c) paleontology
d) primatology

539.

What is the capital city of China?

a) Beijing
b) Shanghai
c) Guilin
d) Suzhov

540.

Which instrument is not a stringed instrument?

a) guitar
b) harp
c) lute
d) saxophone

541.

What is the former name of the country Bangladesh?
a) Kuwait
b) East Palestine
c) Belarus
d) Upper Volta

542.

Which U.S. space probe was sent out to explore Mars?
a) Pioneer 10
b) Mariner 9
c) Magellan
d) Voyager 2

543.

Which famous music hall first opened in 1932?
a) Moulin Rouge
b) Radio City
c) Folk City
d) Grand Ole Opry

544.

Which god of Ancient Egypt is pictured as a jackal-headed man?
a) Anubis
b) Osiris
c) Ammon
d) Geb

545.

Which is false?
a) a barometer measures human body temperature
b) clouds are water vapor that float in the air
c) stalactites grow downward from a cave's roof
d) a volcano is a crack in the earth's crust

546.

Which of these personalities is famous for writing drama?
a) Samuel Beckett
b) George Gershwin
c) Christopher Wren
d) Pablo Neruda

547.

Which South American country shares a border with Panama?
a) Venezuela
b) Columbia
c) Ecuador
d) Peru

548.

A glockenspiel is a
a) percussion instrument
b) wind instrument
c) stringed instrument
d) none of the above

549.

Which of the Four Horsemen of the Apocalypse carries a scale?

a) War
b) Famine
c) Death
d) Pestilence

550.

Who said, "Study the past if you would divine the future"?

a) Seneca
b) Confucius
c) Shakespeare
d) Buddha

551.

Who wrote *The Last of the Mohicans*?

a) James Fenimore Cooper
b) Herman Melville
c) Herman Hesse
d) Jack London

552.

Who said, "These are the times that try men's souls"?

a) Ben Franklin
b) Paul Revere
c) Alexander Hamilton
d) Thomas Paine

553.

What is the official language of the Republic of Botswana?
a) French
b) English
c) Setswana
d) Belgian

554.

Who was Elizabeth Blackwell?
a) the first woman to qualify in medicine in the U.S.
b) a suffragette
c) a human rights activist
d) a Victorian author

555.

Which god of Ancient Egypt has the head of a hawk and is a sun god?
a) Set
b) Horus
c) Osiris
d) Nut

556.

Which animal must constantly move to stay alive?
a) sloth
b) shark
c) spider
d) octopus

557.

What was the nickname of Henry Ford's model T?
a) Tin Lizzie
b) Tin Whistle
c) Tin Pan Alley
d) Tiny Tim

558.

What is the phobia astraphobia a fear of?
a) stars
b) sound
c) thunder and lightning
d) glass

559.

Who performed the first successful human heart transplant operation?
a) Alexis Carrel
b) Alexander Fleming
c) Christiaan Barnard
d) Sigmund Freud

560.

Where is the Nile River?
a) Libya
b) Chad
c) Egypt
d) Saudi Arabia

561.

Who wrote the song, "Semper Fidelis" for President Chester A. Arthur?
a) George M. Cohan
b) John Philip Sousa
c) George Gershwin
d) Aaron Copland

562.

In a classic orchestra configuration, where are the first violins relative to the conductor's podium if you are facing the orchestra?
a) rear
b) left
c) right
d) center

563.

What is Margaret Louise Sanger known as?
a) an advocate for birth control
b) an advocate for human rights
c) an ecologist
d) a biologist

564.

Which style of government is "by the people" and "for the people"?
a) despotic
b) democratic
c) autocratic
d) communistic

565.

Who are Billy Graham, Lao-tzu, and Joseph Smith?
a) physicists
b) religious leaders
c) architects
d) composers

566.

Where was the first performance of Rossini's *The Barber of Seville* performed in 1816?
a) Rome
b) London
c) Vienna
d) Paris

567.

Which of these animals is highest on the food chain?
a) bear
b) fish
c) insect
d) worm

568.

What is the former name of the country of Myanmar?
a) Burma
b) South West Africa
c) Nyasaland
d) Portuguese Guinea

569.

If you are playing poker, what are the odds of getting a royal flush?

a) 649,739 to 1
b) 46 to 1
c) 20 to 1
d) 254 to 1

570.

What were the 1890s known as?

a) Gay Nineties
b) Naughty Nineties
c) Nice Nineties
d) New Nineties

571.

In which century was the Minuet a popular dance?

a) 16th
b) 17th
c) 18th
d) 19th

572.

Where was Mozart's opera *The Marriage of Figaro* first performed in 1786?

a) Paris
b) Turin
c) Vienna
d) Prague

573.

What do these plants have in common: flypaper plant, venus flytrap, and butterwort?
a) all are carnivores
b) all are fungi
c) all are moss
d) all store water

574.

Which canals are not in the U.S.?
a) Erie
b) Sault St. Marie
c) Suez
d) Grand

575.

Which is not an input device on a computer?
a) keyboard
b) printer
c) mouse
d) scanner

576.

In Internet lingo, what does LOL mean?
a) laugh out loud
b) lots of luck
c) lots of love
d) none of the above

577.

Who developed the first vaccine for polio?
a) Margaret Louise Sanger
b) Jonas Salk
c) Walter Reed
d) Louis Pasteur

578.

Who built the first motion picture film studio?
a) Charlie Chaplin
b) Mary Pickford
c) Thomas Edison
d) Alexander Graham Bell

579.

Which is not a play by Tennessee Williams?
a) *The Glass Menagerie*
b) *Night of the Iguana*
c) *Cat on a Hot Tin Roof*
d) *Desire Under the Elms*

580.

Which opera was composed by an American?
a) *Porgy and Bess*
b) *Don Giovanni*
c) *Otello*
d) *Aida*

581.

Where in the human body is the thyroid gland?
a) abdomen
b) skull
c) neck
d) pelvis

582.

What kind of animals eat plants?
a) carnivores
b) omnivores
c) herbivores
d) none of the above

583.

Which album by Celine Dion won the 1996 Grammy Award?
a) Falling Into You
d) Time Out of Mind
c) Unplugged
d) The Bodyguard

584.

Who discovered the North Pole in 1909?
a) Sir Edmund Hillary
b) Admiral Peary
c) Lewis and Clark
d) Byrd and Bennett

585.

Which clown jumped *out of the inkwell?*
a) Bozo
b) Koko
c) Pennywise
d) Chocolat

586.

In the human body, where is the carotid artery located?
a) leg
b) neck
c) arm
d) foot

587.

In which century was Charles Darwin's book *Origin of the Species* published?
a) 1600s
b) 1700s
c) 1800s
d) 1900s

588.

In which movie did Rudolph Valentino star?
a) *The Great Train Robbery*
b) *The Sheik*
c) *The Covered Wagon*
d) *What Price Glory?*

589.

Which major American playwright won the Pulitzer Prize four times and won the Nobel Prize for Literature?
a) Edward Albee
b) Arthur Miller
c) Lillian Hellman
d) Eugene O'Neill

590.

Which group led by Lenin forced Czar Nicholas II to abdicate the throne in 1917?
a) Bolsheviks
a) Communists
c) Nazis
d) Fascists

591.

Which country singer lost many band members in a plane crash?
a) Shania Twain
b) Dolly Parton
c) Naomi Judd
d) Reba McEntire

592.

Who directed the classic films *Paths of Glory* and *Lolita*?
a) Orson Wells
b) Stanley Kubrick
c) Mike Nichols
d) John Ford

593.

Which type of gift is customary for someone's sixth wedding anniversary?
a) wood
b) sugar
c) leather
d) cotton

594.

Which region of the U.S. is the state of the New York in?
a) New England
b) Middle Atlantic
c) South Atlantic
d) none of the above

595.

What made the Blizzard of 1888 an event never to be forgotten in the history of New York?
a) it snowed for 36 hours
b) it snowed for 48 hours
c) it snowed for five days
d) it snowed for seven days

596.

When was the U.S. Military Academy at West Point founded?
a) 1795
b) 1802
c) 1846
d) 1903

597.

Which famous person came from Colorado?
a) Benedict Arnold
b) Titanic survivor, the "Unsinkable" Molly Brown
c) Edgar Rice Burroughs
d) Daniel Boone

598.

Which state's nickname is the Volunteer State?
a) Kentucky
b) Hawaii
c) California
d) Tennessee

599.

Who said, "familiarity breeds contempt—and children"?
a) Ogden Nash
b) Mark Twain
c) Oscar Wilde
d) Noel Coward

600.

What is Jacques Cousteau well-known for?
a) he invented the aqualung
b) he pioneered underwater photography
c) he was a naval officer
d) all of the above

601.

Who was Jane Addams?
a) a biologist
b) a social reformer
c) an ecologist
d) a suffragette

602.

As of 1998, which of these small businesses in the U.S.
had the most franchises?
a) Dunkin Donuts
b) 7-Eleven
c) KFC
d) Snap-on Tools

603.

Who established a fascist-dictatorship in Italy
in the 1920s?
a) Benito Mussolini
b) the Black Shirts
c) Marshal Badoglio
d) Victor Emmanuel III

604.

What happened in 1906 in San Francisco?
a) the city was destroyed by fire
b) the city was destroyed by an earthquake
c) the city was destroyed by rioters
d) the city was flooded

605.

How many days were American hostages held in captivity during the Iran Hostage Crisis?
a) 350
b) 444
c) 450
d) 500

606.

How much money will the next president earn annually since congress voted in 1999 to double the salary?
a) $100,000
b) $200,000
c) $300,000
d) $400,000

607.

Who said, "Every crowd has a silver lining"?
a) P.T. Barnum
b) W.C. Fields
c) Charlie Chaplin
d) Franklin D. Roosevelt

608.

Who established the American Dance Theater in New York City in 1958?
a) Martha Graham
b) Alvin Ailey
c) Isadora Duncan
d) George Balanchine

609.

As of 1998, which of these small businesses in the U.S. had the fewest franchises?
a) Blockbuster Video
b) GNC Franchising
c) TCBY Treats
d) Super 8 Motels

610.

How many commercial nuclear power plants are there in South Carolina?
a) 5
b) 4
c) 7
d) 3

611.

Who said, "Speak softly and carry a big stick"?
a) Harry Truman
b) Dwight D. Eisenhower
c) Theodore Roosevelt
d) Ulysses S. Grant

612.

Which was the Beatles' last album together?
a) A Hard Day's Night
b) Abbey Road
c) The White Album
d) Help!

613.

Who said, "Despair ruins some, presumption many"?
a) Ben Franklin
b) Robert Frost
c) Ralph Waldo Emerson
d) Mark Twain

614.

Who was the first to be honored with the title Lord?
a) John Gielgud
b) Lawrence Olivier
c) George Martin
d) Paul McCartney

615.

What is the capital city of Alaska, the largest state in the U.S.?
a) Anchorage
b) Juneau
c) Fairbanks
d) Kodiak

616.

Which character was created by author Raymond Chandler?
a) Philip Marlowe
b) Sherlock Holmes
c) Miss Marple
d) Father Brown

617.

How many commercial nuclear power plants are there in New York?
a) 6
b) 10
c) 12
d) 13

618.

What are deficiency diseases caused by?
a) genes
b) lack of vitamins
c) viruses
d) aging

619.

What is the all-time top-selling video in the U.S.?
a) *Toy Story*
b) *Forrest Gump*
c) *Titanic*
d) *The Lion King*

620.

Which was not a dynasty of China?
a) Zhow
b) Han
c) Shang
d) Valois

621.

An archipelago refers to
a) a shallow pond
b) a group of islands
c) a narrow, deep-walled canyon
d) a small bay or inlet

622.

Which horse won the 1998 Kentucky Derby?
a) Skip Away
b) Real Quilt
c) Silver Charm
d) Charismatic

623.

Which band did Billie Holiday sing with in 1933?
a) Count Basie's
b) Duke Ellington's
c) Benny Goodman's
d) Glenn Miller's

624.

Who said, "Among mortals, second thoughts are wisest"?
a) Aristotle
b) Mark Twain
c) Euripides
d) Ralph Waldo Emerson

625.

Who took control of the Communist Party in Russia after the death of Lenin?
a) Joseph Stalin
b) Leon Trotsky
c) Nikita Khrushchev
d) Leonid Brezhnev

626.

Which movie stars Victor Mature as a promoter who gets framed for murder?
a) *The Robe*
b) *My Darling Clementine*
c) *I Wake Up Screaming*
d) *Kiss of Death*

627.

Who founded the first American library in 1731?
a) Ben Franklin
b) George Washington
c) Abraham Lincoln
d) Paul Revere

628.

Where was the first "test tube" baby born?
a) Australia
b) France
c) United States
d) England

629.

Which is a hereditary disease?
a) chicken pox
b) scurvy
c) hemophilia
d) allergies

630.

What is the most commonly used illegal drug in the U.S.?
a) alcohol
b) marijuana
c) cocaine
d) heroin

631.

Which author topped a bestseller list from 1994-1998, five years in a row?
a) Tom Clancy
b) Jean M. Auel
c) John Grisham
d) Stephen King

632.

What is an atoll?
a) a hill or ridge
b) a coral reef that surrounds a lagoon
c) a large mass of moving ice
d) a narrow canyon

633.

What distinction do Forego, Affirmed, and Native Dancer all have in common?
a) each is the name of a fragrance
b) all are cruise ships
c) all are Thoroughbred Horse of the Year award-winners
d) all are names of space probes`

634.

Who said, "He who opens a school door, closes a prison"?
a) Charles Dickens
b) Victor Hugo
c) Eugene O'Neill
d) Oscar Wilde

635.

Frank Sinatra won an Oscar for his role in which movie?
a) *Anchors Aweigh*
b) *On The Town*
c) *Ocean's Eleven*
d) *From Here To Eternity*

636.

Which state in the U.S. has the most commercial nuclear power plants?
a) New York
b) California
c) Illinois
d) Pennsylvania

637.

Where was Jonas Salk—who developed the first vaccine against polio—from?
a) England
b) United States
c) Australia
d) Germany

638.

Which was the most popular TV show during the 1998-99 season?
a) *Jesse*
b) *Touched by an Angel*
c) *ER*
d) *Frasier*

639.

Which is the all-time most-rented movie video in the U.S.?
a) *Pretty Woman*
b) *Top Gun*
c) *The Lion King*
d) *Home Alone*

640.

Which is the world's biggest natural lake?
a) Caspian Sea
b) Lake Victoria
c) Lake Superior
d) Aril Sea

641.

Where was the first skeleton of a Neanderthal found in 1856?
a) France
b) Germany
c) Africa
d) England

642.

Which movie won the 1998 Academy Award for Best Cinematography?
a) *Shakespeare in Love*
b) *Saving Private Ryan*
c) *Life is Beautiful*
d) *Affliction*

643.

In what year was U.S. President John F. Kennedy assassinated in Dallas, Texas?
a) 1962
b) 1963
c) 1964
d) 1965

644.

Which event pulled the U.S. into World War II?
a) the bombing of Pearl Harbor
b) Germany's invasion of France
c) Hitler's takeover of Germany
d) Germany's bombing of England

645.

In 1971, when it was first introduced, how much did a pocket calculator cost?

a) $10
b) $50
c) $150
d) $200

646.

Who was the successor to the president after the resignation of Richard M. Nixon?

a) Jimmy Carter
b) Gerald Ford
c) Ronald Reagan
d) George Bush

647.

Which is the customary gift for someone's thirtieth wedding anniversary?

a) coral
b) lace
c) ruby
d) ivory

648.

Who was the star of these movies: *Hud*, *Harper*, and *Cool Hand Luke*?

a) George Kennedy
b) Paul Newman
c) Walter C. Scott
d) Kirk Douglas

649.

Where is the tallest building in the world?
a) Chicago
b) Kuala Lampur
c) Shanghai
d) New York

650.

Where are the Apennine Mountains?
a) Spain
b) France
c) Italy
d) Switzerland

651.

According to the American Film Institute, which actor is the top-ranking screen legend?
a) Humphrey Bogart
b) Marlon Brando
c) James Stewart
d) Cary Grant

652.

Which horse is not a Triple Crown winner?
a) War Admiral
b) Citation
c) Secretariat
d) Seabiscuit

653.

Which was the most successful Rogers and Hammerstein musical?
a) *Oklahoma*
b) *Carousel*
c) *The Sound of Music*
d) none of the above

654.

During whose presidency did the Cold War between the U.S. and Russia end?
a) Ronald Reagan
b) George Bush
c) Richard Nixon
d) Bill Clinton

655.

How many people inhabit the world as of 1999?
a) 4 billion
b) 5 billion
c) 6 billion
d) none of the above

656.

Which icon of baseball was known as "The Yankee Clipper"?
a) Babe Ruth
b) Roger Maris
c) Hank Aaron
d) Joe DiMaggio

657.

Which U.S. Service Academy was founded last?
a) Air Force Academy
b) Merchant Marine Academy
c) Coast Guard Academy
d) Naval Academy

658.

Which popular singer of the 1980s was known by the nickname "The Boss"?
a) Elvis Costello
b) Darryl Hall
c) Bruce Springsteen
d) Bob Marley

659.

Where is the Ivory Coast?
a) United States
b) India
c) Africa
d) Saudi Arabia

660.

How many member states are in the United Nations?
a) 150
b) 188
c) 200
d) 250

661.

Which was the first satellite to orbit the earth?
a) Corona
b) Explorer I
c) Nimbus I
d) Sputnik I

662.

According to the American Film Institute, which actress is the top-ranking screen legend?
a) Bette Davis
b) Ingrid Bergman
c) Audrey Hepburn
d) Katharine Hepburn

663.

What was the name of the 1975 stage musical version of L. Frank Baum's *The Wizard of Oz*?
a) Oz
b) The Wiz
c) The Great Oz
d) The Wonderful Wiz

664.

Which president signed into law the Social Security Act?
a) Franklin D. Roosevelt
b) John F. Kennedy
c) Lyndon B. Johnson
d) Jimmy Carter

665.

Which is a deficiency disease?
a) cystic fibrosis
b) scurvy
c) measles
d) lead poisoning

666.

Which single TV show was the top-rated in history?
a) *M*A*S*H* (The Final Episode)
b) *Dallas* (Who Shot J.R.?)
c) *Roots*, part 8
d) *The Bob Hope Christmas Show*

667.

From which country are most tourists to the U.S.?
a) Mexico
b) Japan
c) Canada
d) Germany

668.

Who won the 1999 Tour De France?
a) Marco Pantini
b) Lance Armstrong
c) Jen Ullrich
d) Bijarne Riis

669.

Who said, "Home is where the heart is"?
a) Socrates
b) Tennyson
c) Pliny the Elder
d) Voltaire

670.

Which song is Lena Horne best known for?
a) Bill
b) Stormy Weather
c) Over the Rainbow
d) Tenderly

671.

Which tunnel is not located in New York?
a) Holland Tunnel
b) Lincoln Tunnel
c) Second Street Tunnel
d) Brooklyn-Battery Tunnel

672.

Which is not true?
a) turtles are reptiles
b) tortoises are quick-moving turtles that live in water
c) the largest turtle is the sea turtle
d) some turtles are endangered

673.

Where was Valley Forge—the camp set up by General George Washington and the Continental Army—located?
a) New York
b) Massachusetts
c) Pennsylvania
d) Connecticut

674.

Which city is "Canada's Gateway to the Pacific"?
a) Montreal
b) Quebec
c) Vancouver
d) Ottawa

675.

What was Cornelius Vanderbilt's nickname?
a) Captain
b) Commodore
c) General
d) Sir

676.

Who said, "Our necessities never equal our wants"?
a) William Blake
b) Jonathan Swift
c) Ben Franklin
d) William Shakespeare

677.

Which was the longest-running national network series of all time?

a) *Gunsmoke*
b) *60 Minutes*
c) *Walt Disney*
d) *The Ed Sullivan Show*

678.

To which destination do most U.S. tourists travel?

a) Canada
b) Mexico
c) United Kingdom
d) Italy

679.

Which was not a Roman emperor?

a) Nero
b) Augustus
c) Charlemagne
d) Titus

680.

Who is best known for the song People?

a) Barbra Streisand
b) Kate Smith
c) Judy Garland
d) Marlene Dietrich

1. **(c)** 9
2. **(c)** Buffalo, New York
3. **(a)** the Bull
4. **(c)** Australia
5. **(a)** farthest from the sun
6. **(a)** Connecticut
7. **(b)** attempt to set world oil prices by controlling its production
8. **(a)** George Washington
9. **(d)** all of the above
10. **(c)** 7
11. **(b)** sea turtle
12. **(b)** 4
13. **(a)** Star of David
14. **(a)** range of colors
15. **(a)** left
16. **(a)** $5
17. **(d)** Tel Aviv
18. **(c)** Middle Ages
19. **(c)** Braille
20. **(c)** pine beetles
21. **(c)** upper arms
22. **(c)** 15% of the bill
23. **(b)** Austin
24. **(a)** New York
25. **(b)** Richard Chamberlain
26. **(a)** they revolve around the sun
27. **(a)** pony
28. **(b)** 2 p.m.
29. **(b)** semantics
30. **(a)** Rome
31. **(a)** Poland
32. **(a)** north of Oregon
33. **(b)** 206
34. **(a)** shoulder
35. **(b)** standing
36. **(c)** Bermuda
37. **(c)** kwanza
38. **(a)** Vostok
39. **(c)** Sacramento

40. **(b)** Jackie Gleason
41. **(a)** Andrew Jackson
42. **(b)** Sirhan Sirhan
43. **(b)** 4
44. **(b)** Australia
45. **(b)** Africa
46. **(d)** basketball
47. **(a)** Theodore Roosevelt
48. **(b)** malaria
49. **(c)** John F. Kennedy
50. **(b)** frog
51. **(c)** arithmetic
52. **(d)** all of the above
53. **(d)** pediatrician
54. **(a)** of the dinosaur
55. **(b)** Paul Newman
56. **(b)** the Three Stooges
57. **(a)** there is no gravity on the moon
58. **(c)** Mississippi
59. **(c)** Tyrannosaurus
60. **(b)** Isaac Newton

61. **(c)** California
62. **(b)** typhus
63. **(a)** Jimmy Carter
64. **(a)** the currency used in the Vatican is the lira
65. **(c)** acre
66. **(a)** bonnet
67. **(c)** patience
68. **(d)** Crazy
69. **(a)** the moon passes in front of the sun and is between it and the earth
70. **(c)** South America
71. **(d)** Seismosaurus
72. **(a)** Near East
73. **(d)** Jimmy Carter
74. **(c)** Cher
75. **(b)** St. Francis of Assisi
76. **(b)** hepatitis
77. **(a)** braces
78. **(b)** Eddie Murphy
79. **(a)** they give off light

80. **(b)** seismos
81. **(a)** Levi Straus
82. **(b)** duke
83. **(d)** birds
84. **(a)** Madrid
85. **(a)** jaw
86. **(a)** all can be used as home remedies
87. **(a)** Heimlich maneuver
88. **(b)** the Declaration of Independence
89. **(a)** Richie Valens
90. **(c)** white dwarf
91. **(c)** diamond
92. **(c)** and **(d)** a swarm and a grist
93. **(c)** coniferous
94. **(c)** 9 p.m.
95. **(a)** Chinese
96. **(b)** John F. Kennedy
97. **(c)** Bobby Fischer
98. **(b)** Ronald Reagan

99. **(a)** Death Valley, ` California
100. **(d)** Mary Celeste
101. **(a)** Martina Navratilova
102. **(a)** Hanover
103. **(a)** Will Rogers
104. **(a)** Everest
105. **(d)** baroness
106. **(a)** flash flood
107. **(a)** $1 per coat
108. **(b)** Canada
109. **(b)** *Les Miserables*
110. **(b)** telescope
111. **(a)** cucumber
112. **(c)** Saratoga Springs
113. **(a)** Ben Franklin
114. **(a)** all are deserts
115. **(a)** Dallas Stars
116. **(a)** Abraham Lincoln
117. **(c)** the vice president
118. **(c)** ruby
119. **(d)** Middle Ages

120. **(d)** Elizabeth I
121. **(c)** 15% of the bill
122. **(a)** Israel
123. **(b)** Montpelier
124. **(c)** 16
125. **(a)** 4 years
126. **(b)** Madonna
127. **(d)** 3/4
128. **(c)** topaz
129. **(c)** all measure time
130. **(c)** Baton Rouge
131. **(a)** Sheryl Crow
132. **(b)** 12
133. **(b)** 11 p.m.
134. **(c)** 48
135. **(c)** ear
136. **(c)** the Twins
137. **(b)** Mount Waialeale, Hawaii
138. **(a)** Jean-Paul Sartre
139. **(a)** Tony Award
140. **(a)** Patrick Henry
141. **(d)** Kentucky
142. **(d)** Texas
143. **(b)** Marlon Brando
144. **(d)** Arctic
145. **(d)** Chinese
146. **(d)** Germany
147. **(c)** Cubism
148. **(c)** China
149. **(b)** Roger Bacon
150. **(b)** the Great
151. **(b)** September
152. **(c)** avocado
153. **(a)** William Le Baron Jenny
154. **(c)** *Wild, Wild West*
155. **(b)** his fiddler's three
156. **(b)** Mayan
157. **(a)** Pizarro
158. **(c)** a dream
159. **(b)** architecture
160. **(c)** when you put numbers in place order

161. **(b)** Captain Hook
162. **(b)** mineral
163. **(a)** Alexander Hamilton
164. **(b)** feudal
165. **(c)** the speed of sound
166. **(b)** Captain Kangaroo
167. **(a)** the cradle will rock
168. **(c)** the first human launched into orbital flight
169. **(a)** Alaska
170. **(a)** Jefferson
171. **(c)** Titans
172. **(c)** Aztec
173. **(b)** Twinkle, Twinkle Little Star
174. **(a)** all are animals
175. **(b)** Irish
176. **(b)** Stone Age
177. **(d)** *Tightrope*
178. **(c)** in the counting house
179. **(a)** high in the Andes Mountains
180. **(c)** Mayflower
181. **(b)** Alexander
182. **(b)** Gene Hackman
183. **(a)** perigee
184. **(d)** all of the above
185. **(c)** Asia
186. **(d)** Paul Revere
187. **(b)** jazz
188. **(b)** Stone Age
189. **(b)** *The Miracle Worker*
190. **(d)** The Ugly Duckling
191. **(b)** Spain
192. **(c)** Pilgrims
193. **(b)** Vikings
194. **(a)** Boris Pasternak
195. **(a)** lamps in a window
196. **(b)** H.G. Wells
197. **(b)** 1930s
198. **(a)** ziti

199. (c) reptiles
200. (a) the Dept. of Justice
201. (a) Boston
202. (c) octopus
203. (c) Dawn
204. (a) Rudolph
205. (b) the Lost Boys
206. (b) almost 4000 miles
207. (c) Statue of Liberty
208. (d) a note to follow so
209. (a) architect of the White House
210. (a) Frank Lloyd Wright
211. (a) photographing landscapes of the American Southwest
212. (a) McKinley
213. (a) the Great Lakes
214. (a) Ben Franklin
215. (a) Pandora
216. (a) 1912
217. (a) clockwise
218. (c) Rasputin
219. (d) a portion of the screen that contains its own document
220. (a) Tudor
221. (c) January 1, 2001
222. (b) magnifying glass
223. (a) Panama
224. (a) grow fonder
225. (a) Nepal/Tibet
226. (a) John Wayne
227. (b) Victor Hugo
228. (c) Albert Einstein
229. (a) Africa
230. (d) Mead
231. (a) Wilt Chamberlain
232. (b) 27
233. (a) Isaac
234. (b) Martina Navratilova
235. (a) universe
236. (a) a modern American writer

237. **(a)** California

238. **(c)** Nile

239. **(a)** in my opinion

240. **(a)** *The Grapes of Wrath*

241. **(c)** Father's Day

242. **(a)** the president of the U.S.

243. **(a)** Aeschylus

244. **(d)** all of the above

245. **(a)** China

246. **(a)** Tenzing Norgay

247. **(c)** Islam

248. **(c)** Michael Jordan

249. **(a)** 1924

250. **(b)** none

251. **(a)** the melting of the Polar ice caps

252. **(a)** Hershey Foods Corp.

253. **(a)** China

254. **(a)** Dallas Cowboys

255. **(c)** New York City

256. **(c)** Rome

257. **(b)** Pleistocene

258. **(a)** Antigone

259. **(a)** the Boston Tea Party

260. **(b)** Pony Express

261. **(a)** Modred, his kinsman

262. **(a)** Minerva

263. **(b)** 1920s

264. **(a)** Eastern Time

265. **(a)** letters from the Hebrew alphabet

266. **(b)** steamboat

267. **(a)** a farmer's wife who began painting in her 70s

268. **(b)** Copernicus

269. **(c)** religious ecstasy

270. **(c)** Alaska

271. **(d)** Italy

272. **(c)** America's Cup

273. **(a)**, **(b)**, and **(c)** Colin L. Powell, Maya Angelou, and Marian Anderson

274. (b) 5 years
275. (c) Theodore Roosevelt
276. (b) a narrow portion
of the Atlantic Ocean
277. (b) 13
278. (b) W.C. Fields
279. (a) Joseph Smith
280. (a) a world-renowned
trumpet player
281. (a) the Conqueror
282. (b) Birdseye
283. (a) Grand Canyon
284. (b) Hera
285. (c) Cassius Clay
286. (c) bats
287. (b) Oz
288. (c) bear
289. (a) Japan
290. (a) 1900
291. (c) Bering Straight
292. (c) snake
293. (d) New York

294. (d) Wilt Chamberlain
295. (a) Allen Funt
296. (c) Tarzan
297. (b) butterflies
298. (c) Pyramids of Egypt
299. (d) Canada
300. (c) 19th
301. (a) Genghis Khan
302. (a) bubonic plague
303. (b) Jefferson Davis
304. (b) conservation
305. (b) Rocky Mountains
306. (d) 144
307. (a) the Ottoman Turks
308. (a) Nashville, Tennessee
309. (b) great leaders of
Native American
peoples in the U.S.
310. (b) White Christmas
311. (a) Christopher
Columbus
312. (c) the storming of the

Bastille

313. **(c)** all are renowned movie directors

314. **(a)** and **(d)** Sears Tower in Chicago, Illinois and the World Trade Center buildings in New York

315. **(c)** Hoover Dam

316. **(a)** the allied invasion of German-occupied France

317. **(a)** Arizona

318. **(b)** *Samson and Delilah*

319. **(c)** Newt Gingrich

320. **(d)** Reverend Dr. Martin Luther King, Jr.

321. **(a)** 180 degrees

322. **(c)** 4700 years

323. **(b)** discoverer of the vaccine for small pox

324. **(d)** Waterloo

325. **(a)** the Lone Star State

326. **(a)** Austrian Archduke Franz Ferdinand

327. **(a)** Dean Rusk

328. **(d)** Windsor

329. **(a)** IBM

330. **(a)** Toni Morrison

331. **(c)** California

332. **(b)** Thomas Jefferson

333. **(b)** two cent coin of 1864

334. **(a)** acronyms

335. **(d)** with great praise or honor

336. **(a)** Christopher Columbus

337. **(a)** right

338. **(a)** all received a Nobel Prize in Literature

339. **(d)** Newbery Medal

340. **(a)** $100

341. **(d)** Medal of Honor

342. **(a)** Alan B. Shepard, Jr.

343. **(a)** the U.S. Capitol Building

344. **(a)** John H. Glenn, Jr.

345. **(b)** all are endangered species

346. **(a)** 25 years

347. **(c)** cheetah

348. **(c)** Caldecott Medal

349. **(a)** *Casablanca*

350. **(a)** all are venomous snakes

351. **(b)** San Diego Wild Animal Park

352. **(a)** Labrador Retriever

353. **(c)** Methuselah

354. **(b)** Titanic

355. **(c)** *Cats*

356. **(d)** 1962

357. **(d)** Hatsfield Atlanta International

358. **(c)** Dayton, Ohio

359. **(a)** International Radio Alphabet

360. **(a)** troposphere

361. **(a)** 1903

362. **(a)** Ellen Church

363. **(a)** 1947

364. **(a)** *Going My Way*

365. **(a)** with the highest praise or honor

366. **(b)** acronyms

367. **(d)** all of the above

368. **(b)** Michael

369. **(c)** joie de vivre

370. **(b)** tornado

371. **(a)** they are all pen names used by women authors

372. **(a)** Samuel Clemens

373. **(a)**, **(b)**, and **(c)** commitment, embarrass, and millennium

374. **(a)** typhoon

375. (b) 460 inches

376. (c) Lusitania

377. (c) Chernobyl

378. (a) John Wilkes Booth

379. (b) Sara Lee

380. (c) to settle disputes
peacefully and come to
member nations'
defense if necessary

381. (b) Germany

382. (a) James A. Garfield

383. (b) two weeks

384. (a) perihelion

385. (a) meteorite

386. (c) the Ram

387. (a) Hindenburg

388. (c) 1000 years

389. (a) solstice

390. (a) the Crab

391. (a) Greenland

392. (b) Balboa

393. (b) Victoria

394. (c) knee

395. (a) Bette Davis

396. (d) nutrition

397. (b) the Lion

398. (b) Egypt

399. (a) United Kingdom

400. (b) shapes of cars

401. (a) Louis XIV

402. (b) Salvador Dali

403. (c) to provide services
to children of
low-income families

404. (a) Sagittarius

405. (a) femur

406. (b) a social science

407. (b) Bryan Allen

408. (b) *The Jazz Singer*

409. (d) *Green Acres*

410. (a) Ralph Waldo
Emerson

411. (c) Capricorn

412. (d) Mojave

413. **(b)** lower leg

414. **(b)** Kevin Costner

415. **(a)** Voyager 2

416. **(c)** 30 tons

417. **(b)** 12

418. **(b)** Henry Ford

419. **(d)** all of the above

420. **(b)** 1960s

421. **(a)** *The Big Clock*

422. **(a)** constellations

423. **(a)** all are constellations

424. **(c)** Cumulus

425. **(c)** southern tip of South America

426. **(b)** ear

427. **(b)** *Platoon*

428. **(a)** swan

429. **(c)** civil

430. **(d)** Scotland

431. **(a)** Charles I

432. **(b)** American Civil War photographer

433. **(b)** John Huston

434. **(a)** 240 BC

435. **(d)** dragon

436. **(a)** Faye Dunaway

437. **(a)** *Weeping Woman*

438. **(b)** *The Thinker*

439. **(b)** Edward Lear

440. **(b)** boxing

441. **(c)** move a rubber tree plant

442. **(b)** Mariana Trench

443. **(c)** every 76 years

444. **(b)** the Hunter

445. **(a)** northern hemisphere

446. **(b)** Ancient Greeks

447. **(d)** United States

448. **(c)** Africa

449. **(b)** spiral

450. **(a)** Galileo

451. **(d)** Joseph Cornell

452. **(b)** Pluto

453. **(b)** major world battles

454. **(c)** birds

455. **(b)** aurora australis

456. **(a)** Big Bang

457. **(c)** Mercury

458. **(d)** all of the above

459. **(d)** Marx and Engels publish the *Communist Manifesto*

460. **(b)** Rudyard Kipling

461. **(b)** Valentina Tereskova

462. **(c)** a physical science

463. **(a)** Mars

464. **(a)** Saturn

465. **(a)** in orbit around the earth

466. **(b)** 2

467. **(a)** Galileo

468. **(a)** Mercury and Venus

469. **(a)** twice a year

470. **(b)** Star and Crescent

471. **(c)** Triton

472. **(a)** the telescope was invented

473. **(b)** Earth

474. **(c)** 5

475. **(b)** om

476. **(a)** ionosphere

477. **(b)** Year of the Dragon

478. **(a)** lotus

479. **(a)** New York

480. **(d)** International Radio Alphabet

481. **(b)** D

482. **(d)** medicine

483. **(b)** Italy

484. **(b)** 1975

485. **(c)** Jupiter

486. **(c)** coyote

487. **(a)** human cloning

488. **(d)** Rachel Carson

489. **(b)** 1930s

490. **(c)** see you later

491. **(c)** Jean Piaget

492. **(c)** Portrait of Dr. Gachet

493. (a) 1911

494. (c) Portugal

495. (b) *Holiday Inn*

496. (b) Korean War

497. (a) CBS

498. (a) and **(b)** China and Egypt

499. (b) Little Snake

500. (b) Promontory Point, Utah

501. (b) Olds

502. (b) psychology

503. (c) Treaty of Versailles

504. (d) Edward Albee

505. (c) Adriatic Sea

506. (b) 20 to 1

507. (a) *Fantasia*

508. (b) 1931

509. (a) Harry Truman

510. (b) Alan Freed

511. (b) cerebellum

512. (a) Polaris

513. (d) coyote

514. (a) books

515. (d) baritone

516. (c) Kenny Black

517. (b) Brazil

518. (b) 1981

519. (b) Hank Williams

520. (b) Persia

521. (b) Mary Cassatt

522. (a) King Henry VIII

523. (d) Pestilence

524. (b) Cicero

525. (b) Malay

526. (b) thousands of species of bacteria live in a handful of soil

527. (b) hands and feet

528. (c) Lauryn Hill

529. (b) speakeasies

530. (c) types of rocks

531. (a) piccolo

532. (b) Samuel Johnson

533. (a) Arabic

534. (b) Robert Charles Gallo

535. (c) sea horse

536. (c) Alan Greenspan

537. (d) cosmology

538. (a) ornithology

539. (a) Beijing

540. (d) saxophone

541. (b) East Palestine

542. (b) Mariner 9

543. (b) Radio City

544. (a) Anubis

545. (a) a barometer measures human body temperature

546. (a) Samuel Beckett

547. (b) Columbia

548. (a) percussion instrument

549. (b) Famine

550. (b) Confucius

551. (a) James Fenimore Cooper

552. (d) Thomas Paine

553. (b) English

554. (a) the first woman to qualify in medicine in the U.S.

555. (b) Horus

556. (b) shark

557. (a) Tin Lizzie

558. (c) thunder and lightning

559. (c) Christiaan Barnard

560. (c) Egypt

561. (b) John Philip Sousa

562. (b) left

563. (a) an advocate for birth control

564. (b) democratic

565. (b) religious leaders

566. (a) Rome

567. (a) bear

568. (a) Burma

568. **(a)** Burma
569. **(a)** 649,739 to 1
570. **(a)** Gay Nineties
571. **(c)** 18th
572. **(c)** Vienna
573. **(a)** all are carnivores
574. **(c)** and **(d)** Suez and Grand
575. **(b)** printer
576. **(b)** lots of luck
577. **(b)** Jonas Salk
578. **(c)** Thomas Edison
579. **(d)** *Desire Under the Elms*
580. **(a)** *Porgy and Bess*
581. **(c)** neck
582. **(c)** herbivores
583. **(a)** Falling Into You
584. **(b)** Admiral Peary
585. **(b)** Koko
586. **(b)** neck
587. **(c)** 1800s

588. **(b)** *The Sheik*
589. **(d)** Eugene O'Neill
590. **(a)** Bolsheviks
591. **(d)** Reba McEntire
592. **(b)** Stanley Kubrick
593. **(b)** sugar
594. **(b)** Middle Atlantic
595. **(a)** it snowed for 36 hours
596. **(b)** 1802
597. **(b)** Titanic survivor, the "unsinkable" Molly Brown
598. **(d)** Tennesse
599. **(b)** Mark Twain
600. **(d)** all of the above
601. **(b)** a social reformer
602. **(b)** 7-Eleven
603. **(a)** Mussolini
604. **(a)** the city was destroyed by fire
605. **(b)** 444

606. (d) $400,000

607. (a) P.T. Barnum

608. (b) Alvin Ailey

609. (a) Blockbuster Video

610. (c) 7

611. (c) Theodore Roosevelt

612. (b) Abbey Road

613. (a) Ben Franklin

614. (b) Lawrence Olivier

615. (b) Juneau

616. (a) Philip Marlowe

617. (a) 6

618. (b) lack of vitamins

619. (d) *The Lion King*

620. (d) Valois

621. (b) a group of islands

622. (b) Real Quilt

623. (c) Benny Goodman's

624. (c) Euripides

625. (a) Joseph Stalin

626. (c) *I Wake Up Screaming*

627. (a) Ben Franklin

628. (d) England

629. (c) hemophilia

630. (b) marijuana

631. (c) John Grisham

632. (b) a coral reef that surrounds a lagoon

633. (c) all are Thoroughbred Horse of the Year award-winners

634. (b) Victor Hugo

635. (d) *From Here to Eternity*

636. (c) Illinois

637. (b) United States

638. (c) *ER*

639. (b) *Top Gun*

640. (a) Caspian Sea

641. (b) Germany

642. (b) *Saving Private Ryan*

643. (b) 1963

644. (a) the bombing of Pearl Harbor

645. (c) $150

646. (b) Gerald Ford

647. (b) lace

648. (b) Paul Newman

649. (b) Kuala Lampur

650. (c) Italy

651. (a) Humphrey Bogart

652. (d) Seabiscuit

653. (c) *The Sound of Music*

654. (a) Ronald Reagan

655. (c) 6 billion

656. (d) Joe DiMaggio

657. (a) Air Force Academy

658. (c) Bruce Springsteen

659. (c) Africa

660. (b) 188

661. (d) Sputnik I

662. (d) Katharine Hepburn

663. (b) The Wiz

664. (a) Franklin D. Roosevelt

665. (b) scurvy

666. (a) *M*A*S*H* (The Final Episode)

667. (c) Canada

668. (b) Lance Armstrong

669. (c) Pliny the Elder

670. (b) Stormy Weather

671. (c) Second Street Tunnel

672. (b) tortoises are quick-moving turtles that live in water

673. (c) Pennsylvannia

674. (c) Vancouver

675. (b) Commodore

676. (c) Ben Franklin

677. (c) Walt Disney

678. (b) Mexico

679. (c) Charlemagne

680. (a) Barbra Streisand